Tim,
You have been
awesome to have in
class and a witness to
some amazing stories
of you I had many

Million Dollar Moments

How To EXCELerate Your Life in 5 Minute Bursts of Brain Change

DEBORAH L. HALL

Love,
D.L. Hall.

ISBN:10:1500954969
ISBN-13:978-1-500954963

THIS BOOK IS DEDICATED TO:

The oxygen I need to breathe every day
My own priceless Million Dollar Moments

Brianne, Devon, and Tyler

"Deborah Hall shows us the power of our own actions and the tools we can use to shape new thoughts and outmoded beliefs ~ to help us change and create something better for ourselves and our planet."

Tracy Austin, Ph.D.
Licensed Psychotherapist
Toronto, Canada

Deborah's potent message for personal growth instantly provides extremely effective tools for navigating life to your fullest potential. No matter what page you open to, the words will always support your Million Dollar Moment. You will read this book again and again."

Dr. Mitch Tishler
Author, holistic physician and creator of Seeing With Heart ~ A Breakthrough Journey to Inner Peace

"Million Dollar Moments is a wonderful collection of golden nuggets, inspiration, and simple ways to connect to enrich your life and that of others - Enjoy!"

Alisoun Mackenzie,
Author, Heartatude, The 9 Principles of
Heart-Centered Success.

"Deborah Hall educates and enlightens readers through her brilliant crafting of this book. Presented in a straightforward, easy to read manner this will be a guide to experiencing calm moments throughout your life. I highly recommend this book!"

Helen Valleau
Author, A year of possibilities

CONTENTS

WHY I WROTE THIS BOOK

This book was inspired by **YOU!**

Once upon a time I was falling in love, until there I was, one day, falling apart. This is NOT a fairy tale. It was then, in my darkest hour, that I began a journey that would forever alter the course of my life.

I sat down and began sharing with all of YOU, every week, my thoughts and my feelings of what Truth meant to me. The words came pouring out of me and onto the page. I came face to face with the parts of myself that I hadn't embraced and I hadn't accepted. I came face to face with my shadow self which had always been there, lurking in the background.

And I discovered something amazing. Because of YOU, and your encouragement of me, every week for the past four years, I did the very thing I thought I could not do. I wrote this book.

It became a deeply transformative journey, leaving me feeling both raw and vulnerable. I met a deeper part of myself that I didn't know existed. Funny things happen down there where the spirit meets the bone. My soul has been poured onto every page. Through this creative process, I stumbled upon the Truth.

So it is, with "hat in hand" that I share these moments with YOU...this total eclipse of ***my*** heart. It is my deepest desire that YOU uncover for yourself your own "**Million Dollar Moments**" because....what's inside matters.

Go on, **EXCElerate** your life!

ACKNOWLEDGEMENTS

I have been working on this book officially since 2009, and in my mind for my entire life, never daring to dream that this would become a reality.

There are three women, whose unfailing belief in ME, made this book possible ~ Antoinette Grossi, Lynda Brickell, and Kelly Nicholson.

When I think about the support and friendship you have given me over the past five years, I am humbled to the point of overwhelm by your love, generosity, and kindness. You have helped me through these lean years and my own dark night of the soul time and again, in ways too numerous to say; always by my side and steadfast in your support of me. I am honoured to be counted as a friend. You three are tattooed on my heart forever.

I would like to acknowledge as well others who, through their own quiet means have helped to further this passion of mine.

Marie Dorey, you are brilliant! Your very creative mind intuited what I was looking for when you developed branding, videos, and advertising to help move my business forward. Thank you for your wild enthusiasm and encouragement of my dream.

Amy Shotbolt, it takes a very special kind of person to reach out and help me the way that you so compassionately did. Without hesitation. Without question. Time and again. In small ways. In very big ways. You have been here before; of that there is no doubt. You get it. And you have my undying love.

Melanie Davis, your generosity has changed my life! If not for your virtual assistance, I would not have gotten off the ground. Your gentle nature and compassion have helped me to soar.

Myra Scott, watching your own journey of growth, your networking and referrals to my business never ceased to amaze me. Your thoughtful insights and timely notes inspired me to keep going. Thank you. You are the most optimistic person I know!

Joyce Rothney, my long time friend and encourager of my dreams...I love you. You opened your arms and your home to me when I needed a respite from the long days of trudging along. Your quirky ways included a trip to Drumheller where we bumped into Radio Show Host and TV Personality, Marilyn Denis, quite by accident in a small town ~ population 29. And, then on to a private after-party of Prime Minister Harper's. Synchronicities and serendipities always happen with you! I will treasure you and those moments always.

Nancy Cavallin, you are a gem. You are the Memory Keeper and connector of all old friends and have kept stoking those flames to keep the fires alive. Old friends are like warm fuzzy blankets ~ they give you comfort and accept who you are baggage and all. I am eternally grateful to you for keeping me in the loop during all those long days of being out of touch because of my writing.

Lew Bannerman, Scott Aitken, Ted Funger, John Goodish, Stephen Connell, Ted Parks, John Carr, George Kao, Mitch Tishler, you have all lifted me up at different times during this process. Thank you for your optimism, intelligence, humour, courage and, your willingness to share individually, your own vulnerabilities. That scary, hopeful information taught me much. You are beautiful souls that this world needs more of.

My sincere thanks to my editor, Deb Coman who I met, no less through the evolution of Social Media. Our paths were destined to cross. There are no coincidences. You pulled all the pieces together for me in a way that made this book richer and more meaningful.

An enormous thank you to Suzanne Letourneau and Audrey Van Petegem who wrote the best endorsement and most brilliant review any self-published author could dream of and helped me to get through the final stages of this thing called publishing a book.

I thank my very large and loud Pinkney family for shamelessly telling everyone you know to buy your daughter's, sister's, aunt's, cousin's, niece's book. There is no better marketing than great word-of-mouth referrals!

Lastly, I'd like to thank my sister, Pam, who sent me so many messages of encouragement from the other side of this earth plane that I've lost count. You've helped me to embrace who I really am, to find my voice, and to love "me" first before anyone else, but mostly, for giving me butterflies. I miss your beautiful spirit.

CHAPTER ONE

THE CUP'S MORE THAN HALF FULL

"Don't gain the world and lose your soul, wisdom is better than silver and gold."
...Bob Marley

In times of recession, it's hard not to think about money, or lack of it. If we don't have any, we feel as though we are worthless. But, money does not have the ultimate power over our success and happiness. If understood correctly, money is merely a symbol of value. It is a piece of paper. It really has no true worth.

What matters is your soul. WHO YOU ARE will never lose value. You are priceless to those who love you. Your worth comes not from the big house you own, or what you do, or how much money you have. Your worth comes from within.

So, as you walk in the world this week, go forth and give to this planet a kind word, a moment of compassion, or an act of love. These things, so under-valued, are truly the priceless ingredients in the currency of life!

"When you light someone else's path, you see your own more clearly."
...Deborah Hall

It's at a time in history when it looks as if the world is about to implode. There is famine, war, poverty, pollution, fear, fatigue, discrimination, and domination everywhere. Yet, some people still see the beauty; the wildlife, the waterfalls, the majestic mountains, the sunsets. They act in kindness and light the path. They live in gratitude and hope. They've made stuff happen and they've changed lives. They've changed their own lives in the process.

Actually, they are the ones carrying this whole planet. Why not join them?

"Let us rise up and be thankful, for if we didn't learn a lot today at least we learned a little, and if we didn't learn a little, at least we didn't get sick, and if we got sick, at least we didn't die; so let us be thankful."
...Buddha

When you take the time to stop and be thankful for even the littlest of things, it is an energetic acknowledgement of trust and release. You affirm that what has been asked is already done. And, you can move forward in your day with confidence to do the things you were meant to do, knowing that all will be well.

"At times our own light goes out and is rekindled by a spark from another person. Each of us has cause to think with deep gratitude of those who have lighted the flame within us."
...Albert Schweitzer

The best way to live in gratitude is to pass it on. Expressing generosity and kindness to others can keep your thoughts focused on the positive. When you do this, you not only put forth a wave of good energy to others, but that energy comes back to you in similar form. This week when you take the time to train your mind to be thankful, you create a cycle where optimism soars and an onslaught of serendipities, coincidences, and small miracles will be never-ending!

"This day will never come again."
...Thomas Merton

What a truth! Straight from your heart and into your soul...this truth. You will never again be sitting in your office, or at home, in just the way you are now.

This week, use this reflection to take you deeper into the values that matter and away from dwelling on the insignificant and the useless. Spend time each day with thoughts that bring light to your soul.

You are a spiritual being and there are such gifts within your soul just waiting to be shared. Does that make your entire flippin' day or what?

"The soul would have no rainbows, had the eyes had no tears."
...John Vance Cheney

Be grateful for the challenges that life has thrown at you. It's there where life teaches you the lessons you needed to learn in order to grow. It accesses a wisdom that would not be there, otherwise.

Accept these challenges and ultimately embrace them. For you will experience life with a much greater intensity that you would have, otherwise. It's truly what adds colour to the palette of your life.

"Blessed are those who are cracked, for they are the ones who let in the light."
...Groucho Marx

Isn't it so much fun to laugh? I mean, that deep down belly laugh that leaves you begging for it to stop because you just know your face is gonna fall off if it doesn't?

So many times we take ourselves too seriously. We stress about missing the bus, or missing a deadline. But, it's those people you meet along life's way who have the uncanny ability to make your tummy ache with laughter; it's those people who encourage you to let that silliness in ...they are the ones who allow us to crawl out from that dark underbelly of the world and see the light.

Yep. "Pop Goes the World"...and that's just how I roll.... "I'm sexy and I know it"....uh huh.

"Laughter is like jogging on the inside. Exercise your 'innards' every day."
...Unknown

Sometimes it just sneaks up on you. There you are, quietly going about your business and WHAM! Somebody comes along and pulls your friend's pants down right in front of you! You didn't expect it, weren't looking for it, but there it was....that fun-loving gladiator of the Universe making you erupt way down deep in your belly; making you laugh so hard that you need them to stop so you can catch your breath!

Laughter. It's a natural high. It's good medicine. Having fun and being happy is your birthright. It's sooooo healthy for you.

Oh, and by the way...you float my boat....stock my laughing...shine my armour...are my apple a day! Boom-chica-boom...

"Laughter is the sound of the soul dancing. My soul probably looks like Fred Astaire."
...Jarod Kintz

I love to laugh! It's irresistibly contagious! I can laugh just listening to someone else laughing. I may have no idea what they're laughing at, but it just looks so delicious that I have to take a bite!

Just think about the people in your life who you love. I bet each and every one of them has the capacity to make your belly ache from laughter!

If you wish to glimpse inside a human soul and get to know someone, watch them laugh. If they laugh well, chances are they're a good person.

Oh, my! Gotta go 'cuz...You make me feel like dancin'...

"Every person from your past lives as a shadow in your mind. Good or bad they all helped you write the story of your life, and shaped the person you are today."
...Doe Zantamata

I am who am I today because of the people in my life! How cool is that!! The lessons learned from these people have been nothing short of astounding.

To all you people who have made an impact in my life – and you know who you are – I thank you. All you nurturers, supporters, mentors, bullies, liars, cheaters, funny, loving, sensitive souls....I applaud you.

For my soul has grown immensely because of you. And, I walk with peace in my heart, laughter in my spirit, and my head held high.

The lessons I have learned...I have learned well. I am Calm Today because of you.

"The fact that I can plant a seed and it becomes a flower, share a bit of knowledge and it becomes another's, smile at someone and receive a smile in return, are to me continual spiritual exercises."
...Leo Buscaglia

That, and the pure freedom of wind whipping through your hair as you stick your head out the car window...or chasing little children round and round the table only to tackle them in a big bear hug and smother them with kisses...or the utter joy of seeing bright copper kettles and whiskers on kittens and other endless serendipities that transform your life in magical ways.

Ahhh yes, these simple pleasures really are a feast for the soul. Something to be grateful for. So, let the dining begin.

You make me feel like Dancing. Dancing In the Street. Dancing in Moonlight. You Should Be Dancing. Yeah.

"We have forgotten what rocks, plants and animals still know. We have forgotten how to be...to be still, to be ourselves, to be where life is: Here and Now." ...Eckhart Tolle

I was sitting in my garden (literally) the other day, when most people were at work. The neighbourhood was quiet. Something like the lake is in the early morning dawn. Calm. Still. And, I dug. With my hands. In the dirt. Contemplating life. About how I got to be where I am today.

Sitting there with damp soil all around me, I realized with renewed wonder and awe, what an utterly beautiful moment I was in. What a magnificent planet we live on. And just how very blessed I am to be able to appreciate bugs busily gathering food for their homes or worms slowly meandering across their hilly terrain. No bemused moments. Only happiness. And GRATITUDE.

The simplicity of a quiet moment. To be with yourself. To go within. Very, very powerful.

"Another world is not only possible, she is on her way. On a clear day you can hear her breathing."
...Arundhall Ray

New possibilities are exciting! They're also a little scary. While we've been busy chasing that elusive thing we call money, TIME is slipping by. Quietly. This day will never come again.

Have we been putting our focus on the wrong things? Shouldn't TIME, in fact, be more valuable than money? Can't we slow down enough to savour the peaceful, easy feeling of the early morning dew on our lawns or saunter down the street holding the hand of our loved one? Those are indeed the priceless things we have let slide through our fingers while mistakenly trading TIME for money.

In the meantime, life has been passing us by. We're here on this Earth plane for a very short time, all things considered.

If your first step is towards having something for yourself, why not have beauty; have well-being; have appreciation; have gratitude. You will soon start to find that you accumulate such a wealth on an energy level. Not only that, you have the opportunity to then begin to give much of that away...without depleting yourself.

The great thing is that when you hold well-being and beauty in this new world we are creating, you begin to radiate at a level of light that people are very attracted to.

Are you listening to the songs of new offerings That very attraction is going to start to change the world in a huge way and you will soon see very clearly that this, indeed, is a new world worth having.

"Earth and sky, woods and fields, lakes and rivers, the mountain and the sea are excellent schoolmasters, and teach some of us more than we can ever learn from books."
...John Lubbock

Just stop long enough to take it all in. For you see, awareness creates choice and choice creates change.

Stand tall in the knowledge that you are loved, that you matter. And never forget to be in awe of this awesome world we live in.

Be in AWE of this awesome world we live in.

"In the best of times, our days are numbered anyway. So, would it be a crime against nature for any generation to take the world crisis so solemnly that it put off enjoying those things for which we were designed in the first place: the opportunity to do good work, to enjoy friends, to fall in love, to hit a ball, and to bounce a baby."
...Alistair Cook

Go ahead. It's play time. Connect with family, with friends, with strangers. I mean really connect. In truth. In laughter. In love.

Let the veil of trepidation, or fear, fall down off your shoulders and let yourself be seen for who you really are. Be transparent. Be vulnerable. Let people see those perceived flaws. Take that risk of exposing what you think makes you powerful.

You see, our hearts are really much braver now and we are becoming more comfortable embracing the new and the unknown. Just watch our LOVE gathering. It's infectious!

We truly are the solution. Put a little love in your heart. Let the sunlight of your spirit spill out around you. Don't let people pull you into their storm. Pull them into your calm. And, be thankful. For all that you've got.

"To forget how to dig the earth and to tend the soil is to forget ourselves."
...Mahatma Gandhi

It's simple, really. We have forgotten the instructions for how to live on earth. We have forgotten how to connect with the earth in a spiritual way, a simple way. To honour it. To cherish it. For, you see, everything is spiritual. Everything has a spirit.

Take our own DNA, for instance. Did you know that the DNA of man is the same DNA as in the tree? Think about it. The tree breathes in what we exhale. We need what the tree exhales. In other words, we have a common destiny with the tree. And that's just one example.

Here's another: Our bodies are made up of 95% water and so it stands to reason that, in order for us to stay healthy, we need to drink good water. Water is sacred. Air is sacred.

It is so important for us to remember that we are all from the "earth." And, when the earth, the water, the atmosphere are corrupted, it creates its own reaction. Mother Earth is reacting right now and is in the process of re-balancing herself from all the damage that's been done to her.

The time is now to tend the soil. Learn how to plant something. That's the first connection. Treat all things as spirit.

It's really about learning to love and care about the small things. It's about honouring our Mother Earth. Small things matter. We matter.

"One regret dear world, that I am determined not to have when I am lying on my deathbed is that I did not kiss you enough."
...Hafiz

I love each and every one of you. Have I told you that lately? Can you sense a flutter of the gentle kiss I blow in your direction? Can you feel it? Did it land on your cheek? On your forehead? On your lips?

You bring me such joy. You touch my life in deep, profound, unique ways. So much so that my heart wants to leap out of my chest.

I thank you for being YOU. I thank you for the compassion you show to me. I am grateful for those small kindnesses...a thoughtful word, a simple gesture.

As Thoreau puts it, "The question is not what you look at, but what you see." And, I see Your heart. Big and bold and beautiful. I thank you for blessing me with your friendship...with your love.

CHAPTER TWO

BE A DREAM WEAVER

"Imagination is more important than knowledge. Knowledge is limited. Imagination encircles the world."
...Albert Einstein

It takes one idea, one dream, one leap of faith, one friend, one second in time, to change everything forever! As you go about your week, let go and imagine your possibilities. Let it be a preview of life's "coming attractions." Hint....DREAM BIG!

"Life is not about finding yourself, it is about creating yourself."
...George Bernard Shaw

Make a dream for yourself. Picture it with as much clarity as possible. Make clear in your mind what the outcome will be. Then, completely forget how, when, or where.

Just think what you know to think, say what you know to say, and do what you know to do. Every day. Lots and lots. And watch the magic begin.

"God have mercy on the man who doubts what he's sure of."
...Bruce Springsteen

Whenever you sense something to be right and true... stop. Pay attention to that "gut" feeling. Don't hesitate. Don't second guess yourself.

Take a deep breath and step into it, for you have accessed the ancient wisdom of the universe. It has always been there. It's been there waiting to speak, waiting for you to hear. Quietly. Sometimes, as only the soft breath of a whisper. Not once will that wisdom fail you. Ever.

"Truth is the only safe ground to stand on."
...Elizabeth Cady Stanton

In many, many ways, truth is intuitive. We know it when we see it. We recognize it, we instinctively feel it. There may be no hard evidence to back something up, but when it is the truth, we don't need evidence....we understand it without explanation.

"Wag More. Bark Less."
...Unknown

Believe in those dreams you have for yourself! Get excited. 'Cause that's the way it is with dreams. They scratch at your door looking for attention.

You can see them through the window jumping up and down, trying to get in. Looking for a home. They might go away if you ignore them. Wrong. There they are still there when you open the door. Panting.

Smiling. Wagging their tails.

This week, wherever you go...Wag More. Bark Less.

"All truth goes through three stages. First, it is ridiculed. Then, it is violently opposed. Finally, it is accepted as self-evident."
...Schopenhauer

The truth may take some work to grapple with. You may want to deny it. You may want to go in another direction. But, here's what's wild about the truth....your preferences or biases do not determine what truth is. Silence can, though.

At this very crossroads of humanity, billions of people everywhere are yearning to awaken and understand the truth about themselves. We've reached a period in time when we are all crawling out from the dark underbelly of the old world that we know and we're traveling into a brave new world of light and of truth.

Here's another wild thing: Simultaneously, there are teachers cropping up all over this planet who can help to heal those in need through simple conversation.

And, the most unbelievable thing Truth is the great clarifier. It makes life so much simpler. It's really the only safe ground to stand on. Stick with it. You're sooooooo acing this life!

**"Wisdom is knowing the right path to take.
Integrity is taking it."
...M. H. McKee**

True wisdom means honouring the simple things you do, for they take you down the path to where you need to go. Wisdom is acting sincerely and gracefully. It's knowing that your words are powerful and so you choose to keep those words sacred when you make a promise.

Integrity, on the other hand, is who you are when you turn out the light.

"Believe in yourself, and if there are barricades in your way, figure out how to navigate them, or jump over them....or, kick them down."
...Katie Couric

Your soul chose to be here on this planet at this time in history. You have ancient memories to tap into but, with today's overload of information coming at you through technology, you are sometimes starving for wisdom. It's there, though. Just waiting. For you to believe in yourself.

So, this week, figure out a way to do it. To believe in yourself, that is. For when you do, when you realize the mind-boggling depths of love from which you came; when you get a glimpse of the brilliant footsteps you are to leave here making it possible for others to follow; you will kick down those barricades with joy....and smell more flowers, skip more pebbles in a pond, and hold more hands....

Cow-a-Bunga!

"If we did the things we are capable of, we would astound ourselves."
...Thomas Edison

We all have the potential for greatness. And it all starts from the inside, out.

There is a part of the brain that is responsible for all of our feelings, such as trust and loyalty. It is also responsible for all of our decision-making too, but it has no capacity for language. It's where those "gut decisions" come from. They just feel right, but we have a hard time explaining why we did what we did.

We need to learn to "listen" to these "gut feelings," to give them credence. For they are very powerful. They can influence us to do things that seem illogical or irrational. The power of this part of our brain is astounding.

It's a matter of faith. Trust in yourself. Follow your heart and blow your mind!

"There comes a time when the mind takes on a higher plane of knowledge, but can never prove how it got there."
...Albert Einstein

This higher plane of knowledge is so powerful that it can drive behaviour that sometimes contradicts your analytical, rational, and linear thinking of a situation. Often you "follow your heart" or "trust your gut" even when it flies in the face of all facts and figures.

So, follow those dreams, but release any expectations of how those dreams will manifest. Just expect, with every fiber of your being, that they will. In the meantime, while your mind is soaring to new heights, simply enjoy who and where you are right now...for that rush will come soon enough!

"Close both eyes....to see with the other one." ...Rumi

Shhh, now. Quiet. Close your eyes. Be still. Let those runaway thoughts, well, run away. And leave you alone. Just for a moment. Just long enough so that you can get a glimpse into the possibility of a life you can only dream of. With a calm mind. A still mind. A peaceful mind.

Can you see it I bet you could, if you really tried. Just a stray little dream peeking out at you. Telling you..."Come out, come out wherever you are!"

Then, take a snapshot in your mind of the end result you desire. Go ahead. It's really okay to use that third eye of yours. Shuffle that deck and let the magic begin. I'm sure you will see that the Jokers are really not so wild.

Forget about how, when, or where it will happen. See the beautiful life you are meant to have! And then, let the real fun come out to play!

You party animal, you!

"Knowledge is knowing a tomato is a fruit; Wisdom is not putting it in a fruit salad."
...Brian O'Driscoll

Do you remember a carefree time when saying what you mean and meaning what you say was normal? When a handshake meant something A time when water and air were free

That simple wisdom seems to have left our society. We now go into stores and buy water by the boatload. Do we need air in our tires? Why, we just go to the gas station ...and for only a buck, we can buy the air we need. Wow! Really!!

Imagine with all the water we have in our world, some very clever people convinced us that we needed to bottle it and sell it. And air? Why? We need that to breathe! It's always been free as far as we all knew and now....

Where's the wisdom in that? It's as if we all became possessed with the brains of a bug banging against a windshield. And, it's time to take our power back. To think for ourselves and stop the "dumb-down" effect that has been foisted upon us all.

To do that we must get back to basics. Get back in touch with nature because it is there we can see these self-organizing systems at work...a system of knowing itself. A self-organizing system of simple common sense.

It's time to stand tall and turn on your light. Let the sunlight of your spirit loose, for to let out a great light, you've only got to move a small basket. As someone once said, "If the people will lead, the leaders will follow."

"The intuitive mind is a sacred gift and the rational mind is a faithful servant."
...Albert Einstein

Yes, you read that right. Our intuitive, creative, holistic mind has been asleep for far too long following the orders of our rational mind. And it takes a huge effort to bust free from memory, but if you keep relying on your past experiences, all you succeed in doing is applying old solutions to new problems.

Behind all important events in history are found important economic turning points. And we are at such a point in history right now. These times we are in are not about doom and gloom. It's actually a time of great joy and celebration as our Mother Earth, or Gaia-Sophia as she is also known, re-balances herself in preparation for this mass evolutionary movement.

And the way we help Gaia-Sophia, is by tapping into that beautiful, creative, intuitive right side of our brain and allowing ourselves to receive those sacred gifts. Because that's when all that juicy, fun stuff will kick in!

So, just go out there and forget about what the mainstream media is telling us...they want to keep us in fear! That's their job. Well, we have a job to do, too, and it's this: Embrace those niggling thoughts that there must be something better out there...there is! Let your brilliance shine! And, always remember....on the other side of fear...lies freedom!

As for me, I must go....I have a serious game of hopscotch I need to attend to! Oh...skip to my lou my darlin'...

"Magic's just science that we don't understand yet."
...Arthur C. Clarke

Yet, how do we create new science? How do we get started? How do we leave the maze, the labyrinth that we call life on earth to create something new, something better, something magical for humanity? We use the only gift we've all been given that's capable of making this leap: Imagination.

For you see, imagination isn't about content, or knowledge...we are bloated with far too much information and very little wisdom. It's about creating something that wasn't there before. It's about asking questions to which there are no answers.

Most people want content. They don't want power. They want the easy solution that power can bring.

But what if we started using those particles of "possibility" The value of that process alone would create a deeper and wider scope of imagination...which would lead to a different look and feel to the life you're living. Which would lead to a healthier physical body. Which would lead to magic.

Can you see that we just haven't used our imagination in earnest yet For if we do, new roads will appear and we will be the co-creators of some new science in this world...the likes of which we have never seen!

Imagination. It is fueled by one thing. Our hearts. Do you believe in magic? If so, this is your starting gate. IMAGINE!

"I like nonsense. It wakes up the brain cells. Fantasy is a necessary ingredient in living. It's a way of looking at life through the wrong end of a telescope."
...Dr. Seuss

Why am I wearing an eye patch and shouldering a parrot!! Oh yes...phew. It's because I'm on a high seas adventure to get a peek at those purple whales...

No, wait....I'm now wearing a summer smock with a teacup in hand viewing the grand lawn party with a very suspicious eye because I just know those absurd wildflowers are always crashing the party!

Feeling stuck? Re-invent yourself. The world is waiting for you, you know...

Go outside and bounce a balloon. Listen to the music. There is energy in that air! Go ahead, breathe it all in. Remember, messages, information, and inspiration are coming in a big way. Big air. Big sky. What are you taking in? Wake up those brain cells!

"The voyage of discovery is not in seeking new landscapes but in having new eyes."
...Marcel Proust

There is a phrase *Sapere vedere. Sapere* means "knowing how" and *vedere* means "to see." Knowing how to see. When looked at from another perspective, it changes the saying of "Seeing is believing" to "Believing is seeing."

When you have new eyes, you are capable of believing and seeing what others don't. Knowing how to see is key. It's that insight, you know, that ability to see from within, that gives you that edge. It's what we see with the eyes of our heart.

Sight is a function of the eyes, while vision is the role of the heart. Vision allows those limitations of the eyes to be set free. Vision gives you the freedom to think with your heart.

Never let your eyes determine what your heart believes.

CHAPTER THREE

THE SUNNY SIDE OF THE STREET

"You need to own the treasures you find in your soul."
...Deborah L. Hall

Sometimes we need to be still...to move forward. Give...to receive. Cry...to feel the joy. Let go...to stake the claim. Pretend...to make it real. These are gifts. Treasure them. Own them. Use them to feel their love...and to perhaps discover, it was there all along.

"Don't ask what the world needs. Ask what makes you come alive, and go do it. Because what the world needs, is people who have come alive."
...Howard Thurman

Come on, people. Be prepared to be amazed. Feel the joy that your daydreams bring. Be willing to receive good things in your life. Expect miracles. Take those baby steps and don't attach to the details. And most importantly, take a breath of fresh air, saunter, and come alive!

"I'm working on a dream, though sometimes it feels so far away, I'm working on a dream. And I know it will be mine someday."
...Bruce Springsteen

Believe. It's working! Every day it's getting closer. Everything you've ever wanted is inching closer and closer toward you. Everything is starting to click into place. Don't let the events of today dampen your spirits.

When things seem to be taking longer than you thought they would, it just means you have more time. Things couldn't be better than they are now. There's a journey to enjoy!

And, just because you can't see it, doesn't mean there isn't stuff happening...

"If you want one year of prosperity, grow grain. If you want ten years of prosperity, grow trees. If you want 100 years of prosperity, grow people."
...Chinese Proverb

It's time to grow people, don't you think

It's time to wake up from the spell we've all been under and move toward a collective consciousness that is in keeping with our real natures. We've tried it the other way. It doesn't work.

Praise and celebrate your life and the people in it. Act as if what you do makes a difference. It does.

"This little light of mine, I'm gonna let it shine."
...Harry Dixon Loes (1895-1965)

Go on. Leave the door open. Let your sun shine out! Have fun because when you get clear about how wonderful and powerful you really are, wild horses couldn't stop you from taking the humblest of little baby steps every day. Woo Hoo!

And, that light that is within you will reach halfway around the world. You know, like the ripple effect. Just like a snowball on the top of a mountain has the potential to grow HUGE by rolling down the hill, your little light can become a force to be reckoned with.

So, let your light radiate outward, to ripple its way to a universal awakening for us all.

"The test of the morality of society is what it does for our children."
...Dietrich Boenhoffer

We all know the world is undergoing a huge transformation. We all feel it at some level. So, let's all embrace this shift. Find some small way to improve our environment, our education system, our corporate structure, our government. We are that powerful! There is so much possibility!

Ever wonder why it's easier to remember the good than the bad, the laughter than the sobbing It's simple. It's because there are more good times, there are more times of laughter.

You can create some powerful new roads for society. Leave a beautiful legacy for your children. You only have to believe and then take little baby steps every day toward creating a loving, mindful society.

Roll over Beethoven! Rock me Amadeus! Build me up Buttercup!

"So, tell me who do I see when I look in your eyes. Is that you Baby, or just a brilliant disguise"
...Bruce Springsteen

Every day you play different roles, have different lines. What are all these masks that you wear? You wanna know something? There is a secret undamaged person inside each of you and those masks are just the top layer of your disguise.

As you learn and grow, and discover who you really are, your inner strength emerges, and the light, the truth that is inside each of you begins to shine. It is then you will realize that you are complete and whole and perfect just the way you are at this moment. Be brilliant this week....and lose the disguise!

"Success consists of going from failure to failure without the loss of enthusiasm."
...Winston Churchill

Wow! How DO you keep trudging along after many unsuccessful kicks at the can? It's simple, really. Passion. It is when you are so committed to something you are nuts about that your desire is greater than your fear.

This week, if you really believe in something, stick with it. Do your happy dance and keep on keepin' on because it's a funny thing about making a decision. You never seem to have to convince yourself into the right ones.

"You get the best efforts from others not by lighting a fire beneath them, but by building a fire within them."
...Bob Nelson

It only takes a spark. Power, greed, domination, discrimination are what light a fire beneath you, to get you moving. But, the driving force behind that wee light inside of you is passion.

It could be for any number of things....something you'd love to do to make this world a better place, someone you'd love to embrace that would light up their life, somewhere you'd love to visit.

Seek out someone that can inspire you to build that fire within you. Just hold them as your benchmark for all great possibility for yourself.

Come on...it's in there. You know it is...

Winnie the Pooh: "What day is it" asked Pooh.
"It's today," squeaked Piglet.
"My favourite day," said Pooh.

Ah...to live in the present moment. Now, that is powerful. Really, it's all we have if you stop and think about it. There's nothing in your past than can prevent you from being present now. And, if the past can't prevent you from being present now, what power does it have

I gotta go now. Need to skip-to-my-lou and jump in a puddle!

"A good leader inspires people to have confidence in their leader. A great leader inspires people to have confidence in themselves."
...Eleanor Roosevelt

Leadership is an extraordinary experience. It's a humbling experience.

This week, ask yourself these two questions: "What if I imagined that the whole world was watching me and was using me and my life as a model?" and "What would I do differently?"

A leader is not a person who says, "Follow me." A leader is a person who says, "I'll go first."

"Take away my people, but leave my factories and soon grass will grow on the factory floor. Take away my factories but leave my people and soon we will have a new and better factory."
...Andrew Carnegie

With jobs being cut, and people being downsized, there has begun a movement to create something new. And better. People everywhere are really stretching themselves to produce something meaningful for humanity.

There is a wonderful shift occurring in the hearts and minds of the people on this planet. There can be nothing finer than to utilize a business to create a positive change in the world.

As we move into The Age of Consciousness, the gifts that we've developed as children i.e., computers, technology, agriculture, are the gifts we now need to apply to our true purpose. With care. Consciously. To feed our souls. For the betterment of all. Why? Because, a creative, sacred economy is the fuel of brilliance.

"Nothing is more powerful than an idea whose time has come."
...Victor Hugo

Yes, indeed a shift is happening before our very eyes. If you've been paying attention you are catching glimpses of it. It's here. It's there. It's everywhere. The new buzz words are Triple Bottom Line businesses.

Instead of being solely focused on profit, as typical businesses have been in the past, Triple Bottom Line includes People, Profit, and Planet. Companies everywhere are taking up humanitarian causes as a focal point to their business. Advertisers are alerting us to "moving our world forward" or to "drive change."

Some people are waiting for things to get back to "normal." Well, that's not gonna happen. Something much more amazing is manifesting itself! The state of affairs is indeed gravitating in a new direction. It will blow people's minds, for it will create a planet that we can't imagine at this moment!

So, go out there. Be an unstoppable force! Help create the new direction for this planet. Innovate new systems to disrupt those that are no longer working. YOU are that powerful!

"By God, when you see your beauty, you'll be the idol of yourself."
...Rumi

You are an amazing being! Perfect in every way. And, the gifts you have brought to this world...incredible!

Everything you've ever wanted is coming at you. Everything is clicking into place. Don't let the illusion fool you. Don't let the events of today dampen your spirit in any way. Great things are happening and things couldn't be any better than they are now. This is your parade! This is your show! So, kick it into gear and see the perfect you! Shine, baby, Shine.

And, it's quite the Kodak moment too. Happy tears all around. Sniffle. Sniffle.

"The most important decision we make is whether we believe we live in a friendly or hostile Universe." ...Albert Einstein

Do you believe that the Universe doesn't care, or do you believe that the Universe is actually programmed to lift you to your highest place?

Everyone on this planet has gone through tough times. No one is immune. When I look back at some points in my life, sometimes what I thought of as a success was actually a failure, and sometimes what I thought of as a failure was a success. It all depends on your perspective. It wasn't a failure if you learned from it.

So, what is your mindset "Things won't get better for a long time," or "A miracle is on its way." I know this much...any thought that springs from anger, from fear – because that is the absence of Love ...well, it diverts the miracle.

If you would trust the spirit that is within you to have command in your heart...you will have command in your life. And, that change in thinking IS the miracle.

"Ever since happiness heard your name, it has been running through the streets trying to find you."
...Hafiz

Have you been hiding Come out, come out wherever you are. Come out and show everyone the amazing light that is you. Don't you know the world shines every time you smile? Why can't you just smile?

If you've had your foot hovering over the gas pedal, if you've been waiting to feel inspired or wishing you had the courage to take action in some way, start thinking of ways you might harness that energy this week. Go ahead and make some breakthroughs. If you only knew how amazing you really are, you would astound even yourself!

Now...go outside and play!

"No problem can ever be solved from the same level of consciousness that created it."
...Albert Einstein

Take a look today at the storm that is brewing around us. That's right. We are directly in the "Eye of the Shift." Things seem to be calm where we are but the world is, in fact, having a breakdown. Whether you look at climate change, the Boston bombings, genetically modified organisms (GMOs), the Cyprus financial brink, Solar flares (Coronal Mass Ejections or, CMEs), there is, indeed, a massive shift in consciousness happening. We are, in fact, in between worlds. The old world is gone, and we are about to step into a whole new world.

And, that's a good thing. Because people are awakening from the "dumbed down" state of fear we've all been living in. When we all wake up to this, then the killing will stop and peace will return. We have allowed this to happen, since, by our silence, we gave consent.

The key to our success is to move through the trauma and renew our faith in a loving Universe. Find our voice and speak out. We are all powerful beings of Light. See yourself as YOU ARE, not as you were told you are. Stop believing the propaganda. Let us laugh at the attempts to create fear in our minds and look with clear eyes.

Your primary work for this year is to take a vacation and learn to love yourself. Seeing with the heart. Thinking from the heart. That is how the new business world will operate and the way to be truly bountiful.

So. Let us all raise our heart-consciousness and start solving some problems. That is the only way forward.

"The road to enlightenment is long and difficult and you should try not to forget snacks and magazines."
...Ann Lamott, Traveling Mercies

It's important to go within. Yet, 99% of the population still look outward for their source of happiness. You know, things like a new house, a new car, designer clothes at rock bottom prices. They make us feel happy for a while...

The good news is that now, more than at any other time in the history of mankind, it is easier to make the choice to go within and find that treasure that's buried inside of you because the energies on the planet are lifting...are getting lighter.

Take some time this week. Stop paying attention to the weather, to jobs and economics, to the financial changes that are happening all over the world.

Just be aware of being aware and be happy. And, then "Listen to the Music," go out and "Stompa" your feet! Yeah. It's an inside job, for sure...

"Sing because this is a food our starving world needs. Laugh because that is the purest sound." ...Hafiz

It seems like people are still toweling off from the recent storms we've been in. Still unsure of what exactly we are supposed to do next, as nothing seems to make sense anymore.

I suggest you dig through that "Tee-hee Chuckle" Trunk this week. As much as we can learn from our troubles, it's important to learn from our joys, too! Not everything in life needs to be a lesson.

Lighten up, get outdoors, soak up some rays (they're good for you!), fly a kite, jump in a puddle, dance in the rain. And laugh. Definitely laugh.

"I go to nature to be soothed and healed, and to have my senses put in order."
...John Burroughs

Summertime is a wonderful time to reconnect with nature. Gardens offer us the perfect opportunity to help us remember our true selves and our place within the natural world.

As we drift outdoors on a star-filled night to bask in the rays of the moon, we may hear crickets sing or see the glow of fireflies. And, for some reason, these seemingly insignificant sensations can invigorate the body and delight the soul.

Nature has so much organizing power and so much intelligence that you can tap into! Why not see nature with new eyes? Think with your heart. Feel with your mind. For it is then you can experience a whole new level of appreciation, be a witness to a whole universe of miracles.

Nature. What a trigger for your senses! It may even give you a greater sense of honour between the two worlds. Harness that energy and get into the flow. You won't be disappointed.

"There can be no keener revelation of a society's soul than the way in which it treats its children."
...Nelson Mandela

The truth is...the magnitude of what's happening out there is mind-blowing and most people don't even realize what an incredible period we are in.

Children are precious. They are innocent. They bring laughter and wonder and awe with them when they arrive here. Our responsibility is to love and protect them from harm.

You know, there's only one Natural Law of the Universe..." Do no harm to anyone or anything."

We have all been asked to go deep within ourselves and we've gone through both physical and emotional purging. And, some of that purging has been challenging...almost seems as if it will never end.

This process is temporary and is necessary in order to bring us to these new higher states of consciousness. This process will benefit our children greatly.

This future generation will wonder how all of this happened. Keeping a journal of what is happening to you and what you're seeing in the world is important and will be useful to them later on.

Let's all do our part to unite as a community. To watch out for each other, have compassion for each other, and to love our children well.

CHAPTER FOUR

'TIS BETTER TO GIVE

"Namaste" (pronounced nah-mah-STAY)

...is a greeting spoken with your palms pressed together and centered at your heart. The meaning of Namaste is beautiful, that being "the sweetness in my heart and soul honours that same lightness of the Divine in you."

So, as you go about your life this week, whenever you confer, whether face to face, across the miles, with a fellow man, departed loved one, cat, or dog, always speak to the highest within them.

"We make a living by what we get. We make a life by what we give."
...Winston Churchill

By spending oneself, we become incredibly rich. Let's do what we can this week to lift the energy around us....simply sharing a smile can be a tremendous gift to someone! That small token will ripple out around the planet. The power of our energy is incredibly important.

"Too often we underestimate the power of a touch, a smile, a kind word, a listening ear, an honest compliment, or the smallest act of caring, all of which have the potential to turn a life around." ...Leo Buscaglia

Reach out and touch someone this week, for wherever you go, you can transform people with your own unique energy. Seek to make a difference to someone, however small that difference is. You may be astonished to discover just how powerful your light within you shines.

"If you smile at me I will understand, because that is something everybody, everywhere does in the same language."
...Crosby, Stills & Nash

Sometimes you are so busy with life that you are way too serious for your own good. Just think about it. You run around with a cell phone glued to your ear, or you are busy texting the world it seems. You stress about deadlines and dash through shopping malls never paying attention to the people you pass by.

Let's walk down the street this week, or into a room and do some-thing simple. Smile. You sow anonymous benefits upon this planet because it creates a chain reaction. Don't you know that the world shines every time you smile Guess what Your own heart smiles, as well.

"When we help each other, we realize that we're not here to earn God's love, we're here to spend God's love."
...Steve Bhaerman

Of all the "woo hoo!," "yee haw!" moments that come from being happy, the greatest stems from truly helping others. For it is then, when you help others, that a grace kicks in. You know...that feeling of warmth that starts way down in your belly and spreads.

It certainly doesn't hurt either if you have fun while you're doing it. This week, approach helping others with anything that tickles you. You'll gain tremendously rich rewards. You'll see.

Just "Crank up The Volume." "Shake-Shake-Shake." "Twist and Shout."

"In a gentle way, you can shake the world."
...Ghandi

I bet you could do something for someone today, and they would remember it for the rest of their life. In a good way, of course.

Get ready...get set...

"It's one of the most beautiful compensations in life...we can never help another without helping ourselves."
...Ralph Waldo Emerson

Of all the types of "happy," those that are most valuable by far, are those that are derived by helping others, without attachment, and without the desire for personal gain.

It's when you are in service to others that something magical happens. A subtle force that goes beyond logic or reasoning, called Grace. It's that warm feeling deep down inside when you know you've just done something wonderful for someone.

Know this. If something touches the entrance code of your soul, it is remembered forever and transforms everything that comes afterward. That act of kindness to one person ripples out to many more people you are not even aware of.

Find a way this week to be of service to others. It's the highest path of your soul.

"A business absolutely devoted to service will have only one worry about profits. They will be embarrassingly high."
...Henry Ford

What a profound concept. Service. Something that has truly been forgotten in recent years. Manipulation or inspiration in business One gets short term gains, and the other It's wide open.

Unfortunately, in today's world, the reality is that manipulation in business is the norm. Slashing prices, running promotions, using fear or peer pressure...these are all influencers used by companies to get what they need. Why? Manipulations work. They can help a company become successful, but not a single one of them breeds loyalty.

Inspiration though, it's about empathy. It's about putting yourself in someone else's shoes and wanting to help ease their pain. Going out of your way to do what you can to help them, to be of service to them. It's a gift that you give to others and the reward you and your company will reap is loyalty!

This is how service begins. It's priceless.

"We are visitors on this planet. We are here for ninety or one hundred years at the very most. During that period, we must try to do something good, something useful, with our lives. If you contribute to other people's happiness, you will find the true goal, the true meaning of life."
...H.H. The XIV Dalai Lama

You can start by performing some small kindness for someone. When you do, you actually raise the vibration of your own self. For, in doing a good deed, it releases serotonin (that feel good chemical) in your own brain. You feel better.

What's even cooler Not only will you feel better, but so will people watching that act of kindness. Bystanders will be blessed with a release of serotonin just by watching what's going on. How awesome is that

We are all our brother's keepers. It's a jungle out there....Be CARE-FULL.

"We've all been given a gift, the gift of life. What we do with our lives is our gift back."
...Edo

If you know you've received a gift, the natural response is gratitude. Let's start with that.

To give gifts, you need a group, a community. And, you can't have a community as an add-on to a material life. You actually have to need each other.

We are all in this together. We are all connected. Materialism is dead. Consciousness is the root of everything and our inter-connectedness is more apparent than ever.

Humanity is awakening at an ever-increasing speed and your gift is needed now more than ever before! Remember "energy flows where attention goes."

"Do not wait to strike till the iron is hot, but make it hot by striking."
...William B. Yeats

You are all capable of great things. Of moving mountains, of touching lives, of leaving this planet in a far better place than when you got here. All you have to do is start taking baby steps in that direction as scary as they seem. Go on. Just take those few steps and get them over with.

And if you forgot that there was magic or miracles to believe in...well, now dig deep into that nobility of your soul and catch the heat! It's there.

Here's a tip to help you bring that joy to your life faster than you would have ever thought possible. Every day and in some small way, look for a chance to help someone else. Then just watch how HOT that iron will get! "Oh, oh, oh, I'm on Fire...."

"If your actions inspire others to dream more, learn more, do more and, become more, you are a leader."
...John Quincy Adams

At this juncture in history, it is getting harder and harder to find people in positions of authority who inspire us. With so much bad news everywhere...politics, global economy, and health scares, people are drowning in a quicksand of stress. Why not start this week and point yourself in the right direction to climb out of the mire?

Wanna know how? Start by changing the way you see the world. Believe you live in a friendly Universe. And, then start by working harder on yourself than you do on your job.

There is something simple you can do to get going. It is this. Give. Give a smile to a stranger you meet on the street, or, give your child the attention she deserves and craves. Give up to being right, and give to be happy. You see, most people are nowhere near as successful as they wish they were.

The true secret to success is...giving. Changing yourself is changing the world.

"When the suffering of another creature causes you to feel pain...come closer, as close as you can to him who suffers and try to help."
...Leo Tolstoy

Everyone on this planet carries with them some pain. No one is immune. When someone makes you suffer, it is because they suffer deeply within themselves. May their bad manners, or anger, or cynicism become a signal to you.

Give compassion to everyone you meet, even if they don't want it. For, you never know what wars are waging down there where the spirit meets the bone. They don't need our punishment. They need our help.

Remember, some of the most beautiful people this world has ever known are those who have known struggle, and defeat. Loss and suffering. And, somehow they found a way out of the depths of despair. These very people have an appreciation and a sensitivity that fills them with compassion, gentleness, and a loving concern for all.

Beautiful people...do not just happen. They need our help.

"There is a wonderful mythical law of nature that the three things we crave most in life - happiness, freedom, and peace of mind - are always attained by giving them to someone else."
...Payton Conway March

Giving. That really is the secret to success. So many beautiful, wonderful things come your way from serving others. You see, the most valuable gift you can offer humanity is yourself.

Your true worth is really measured by how much more you give in value than what you actually receive in payment. Serve people. And, serve them well. When you care about the welfare of others in an authentic way, your influence just naturally extends in ways you cannot begin to imagine! Watch out for the other person and make your goal about going after what they want one hundred percent!

It will bring you more happiness, more freedom, and more peace of mind than you can ever dream of! It brings new meaning into the old proverb "Give and you shall receive." That's the power of giving.

"To strengthen the muscles of your heart, the best exercise is lifting someone else's spirit when you can."
...Dodinsky

When events happen that stir a deep emotion in us, events such as the death of Princess Diana, a Tsunami, and 9/11...it activates or creates a rational, coherent energy field here on Earth's plane. It has been recorded and read by satellites that during these times a change in the earth's electro-magnetic fields was produced from an outpouring of human emotion.

And, if you all remember for a few days after 9/11, our world was close, closer than we've ever been...and we were a family. Unlike anything we've ever seen.

So, this week let us plant seeds of a new energy. Let us begin a process of strengthening the muscles of our hearts. Of creating a coherent energy field. Let's sow these seeds well and lift up the spirit of everyone you can.

"Do your little bit of good where you are. It's those bits of good put together that overwhelm the world."
...Desmond Tutu

The atmosphere is crackling with change. We are standing at the precipice of a whole new world.

Perhaps you have sensed this shift. It has happened quietly. Slowly. On a very subtle level. And, it began years ago. Remember, the Berlin Wall coming down The fall of the Soviet Union Dictators who have left or are losing their power Former European enemies coming together to form an economic alliance Most of us didn't even notice it. The idea that you could put things together instead of tearing them apart is new.

But, now these old systems are being exposed increasingly every day. Corruption, greed, deception, domination. And we, the people, are gradually bringing the truth to light.

Yes, there is a bridge for us to cross. And, as we cross it, we must leave the old paradigms behind. Because they don't work anymore. So, what can we do

Nourish everyone you meet with kindness. In a gentle way. With compassion. With love. Help to bring humanity closer to the truth. There's power in numbers, you see.

Come on. Let this be your journey to do your little bit of good where you are, to live an inspired life. It will truly be nourishment for your soul. Ready. Set. Go!

"Someone I loved gave me a box full of darkness. It took me years to understand that this, too, was a gift."
...Mary Oliver

Calamity like that cracks you open. It leaves your soul out there for all to see. But, it does something else too. For, when you are in that emotionally exposed, frantically vulnerable state, it gives you the opportunity to take a good, long look. At your life. At yourself. A chance to go within.

You see, vulnerability is the birthplace of breakthrough, of creativity, and of change. In fact, vulnerability is our most truthful assessment of courage.

That is why vulnerability is the new POWER.

And, here's the really cool thing...the great part of this is that, as you begin to become whole and in balance again, there is a warmth, a light that emanates from you. Others will huddle around and they will see it. And they are simply going to follow your light into their own pathway.

Voila! We have not only lifted ourselves up, we have effectively inspired those that empowered us...and empowered those who inspired us.

Oh what a gift we have received...and then quietly given away!

"If nature has made you for a giver, your hands are born open, and so is your heart; and though there may be times when your hands are empty, your heart is always full, and you can give things out of that – warm things, kind things, sweet things...help and comfort and laughter...and sometimes gay, kind laughter is the best help of all." ...Frances Hodgson Burnett ~ A Little Princess

'Tis the season. To share with family, with friends. And, in the true spirit of the season, it's the time to give. Of yourself.

Share your time with a friend. Shovel a neighbour's driveway. Spend some time with an older person...they too, have much wisdom to share with you. If you let them. Give Love everywhere you go.

Give and you shall receive. Much more than you ever dreamed was possible. You see, the most valuable gift you can give, is yourself.

CHAPTER FIVE

COLD IN OUR TRACKS

"Our deepest fear is not that we are inadequate. Our deepest fear is that we are powerful beyond measure. It is our light, not our darkness that frightens us."
...Marianne Williamson

Think of anyone who has achieved great things. Don't you think that they, too, had their own self-doubts, that they, at times, had razors of fear in their heart, a blackness of doom in their chest They didn't have anything you don't.

They just kept showing up. They just kept doing the work. They ignored those lonely and discouraging feelings, uplifted those wondrous moments, and expected a miracle.

"If you think you're too small to have an impact, try going to bed with a mosquito."
...Anita Roddick

Of course you can! Yes, now...this year! That and more! Feel it, imagine it, and then leap off the bridge like your pants are on fire...you'll build your wings on the way down! And, that will just be the tiniest tip of the iceberg. Leap! Don't wait a second more.

"We are the ones that we are waiting for!"
...The Elders OraibiArizona Hopi Nation

Pssssssst! Around the corner, down the bend in the road, in the unseen, the shift on this planet is happening. Just because you can't physically see a flower growing, doesn't mean it's not.

If people could only glimpse the huge potential you have to create an amazing, spectacular life, you would all rise up and embrace those haunting moments of uncertainty, those awesome twists and turns, those bewitching coincidences...the ones that say, "What are the chances of that happening?" with such a fierceness, it would astound even you!

So, what are you waiting for?

"It is not because things are difficult that we do not dare, it is because we do not dare that they are difficult."
...Seneca

You are soooo where you're supposed to be. At this moment. At this time.

So what if you don't have it yet

It's coming. You're gonna get it. You're gonna have it. You're gonna love it!

Enjoying the moment while you wait, is huge! The key is to keep yourself busy while learning to be happy. Because, if you dare, you are poised for the happiest time of your life.

Go ahead. Just do it.

"Here is a test to find out whether your mission on earth is finished: if you're alive, it isn't."
...Richard Bach

Think about something about yourself that gives you discomfort and that is a good place to start. Why? Because it's where you are ripe for growth.

It's an area where you have become lost...forgotten how powerful you really are, and how much you are loved.

And, when you start to examine that something about yourself, you will come to realize that your brilliance was there all along, life is beautiful, and you will give yourself some slack.

And perhaps, you'll then turn down the windows, feel the wind in your hair, smell more flowers, and hold more hands...

"You don't have to see the whole staircase, you just have to take the first step."
...Martin Luther King, Jr.

You already know that to find your own way, you first have to be lost. To feel big, you have to start out small. To find love, you must feel none.

And, when you find yourself lost and alone, look at it like this...any of those feelings are simply a sign that you have made a really, really big dream and its manifestation has already begun. Just take that first step!

"Miracles start to happen when you give as much energy to your dreams as to your fears."
...Richard Wilkins

Do you know what fear stands for? False Evidence Appearing Real.

This week, get out there and give your dreams energy! Remember whatever you fight, you strengthen. Whatever you resist, persists. Whatever you fear, you draw near.

Why not spend your energy this week believing in your dreams ...You just may find a little miracle!

"We are so accustomed to disguise ourselves to others that, in the end, we become disguised to ourselves."
...Francois de La Rochefoucauld

What a completely, utterly, sad statement.

Every day we stop ourselves, or hold back from saying this or that, for fear of being ridiculed. Or, we say something that we think others want to hear. We play roles. We say lines. Can you realize how far-reaching your thoughts and emotions become to affect your health and well being? Every. Single. Time.

This week, dig deep into that raw and unguarded place and discover that strength, that light, that truth that lies inside of you. For it is then that you will realize that you are perfect, just as you are. Yep. No need to hide anymore.

Pump Up The Volume, Hit Me With Your Best Shot, Get Into the Groove, Rock the Boat, Baby...

"If the mountain was smooth, you couldn't climb it."
...Unknown

Think of one area of your life that brings you discomfort and that's where you are ripe for growth! Of course, you may want to stay exactly where you are and that's okay too. To grow IS a bit of a tough go. Each step is a challenge, and the higher you go, the tougher it gets. It's enough to wear you out!

But hear this! Every day, you're getting closer. Everything that you've ever wanted is being pressed toward you. The air is getting clearer, the sky is getting brighter. Everything is clicking.

Don't let the events of today dampen your spirits. Just show up, be present and let events unfold. And when you've reached the top of that mountain, the part where that awesome view is, well...it's then you'll begin to climb.

"You know sometimes all you need is 20 seconds of insane courage. Just literally 20 seconds of embarrassing bravery. And, I promise you, something great will come of it."
...from the Movie "We Bought a Zoo"

There comes a time in your life when you courageously take a stand for yourself against those who have behaved irresponsibly and in spite of the repercussions. This is a good thing.

And, if you are valiant enough to make it your focus, against all odds, against the temptation to give in, you will come to realize that it's not so much about overcoming your fear, as it is about not settling for less. And, that's when every corner of the Universe will open to create clarity, to transform your life. Yes. The winds will be blowing... Because, on the other side of fear, lies freedom.

Ride on, brave heart...

"At first people refuse to believe that a strange new thing can be done. Then they begin to hope it can be done. Then, they see it can be done. Then, it is done and all the world wonders why it was not done centuries ago."
...Frances Hodgson Burnett

We are living in a world that is confusing and can be overwhelming. You can say "I can't wait 'til things get back to normal," but what you see out there today....this is the new "normal" now.

You see, we've been led to believe in a world of scarcity. A world that deemed only the strong survive, and only the very select few find success. The lens we viewed the world with for the past 150 years is now buckling. Yet, when we disrupt old patterns, new worlds emerge.

And, the easiest way to escape from a problem is to solve it. The way we see through those lenses is the way we will solve every problem, every crisis. Running away from any problem only increases the distance from the solution.

New discoveries are helping us to build a new lens. So, let go of the pain of the past and send it your love. Honour it for what it taught you, the lessons learned, the compassion gained, the strength it gave you. Make the space for something new. YOU deserve the peace it will bring.

'Cause there is sooooo much to be excited about. All you need to do is believe that a new world, a better world can be set in motion, and your belief will help to make that happen.

"We can't, We must not lose this sense of possibility because in the end, it's all we have." ...Unknown

Isn't it interesting how endings can become beginnings? We live in such a fear-based society that most of us have forgotten, and let slip away, our sense of possibility.

We live in fear of poverty, fear of loneliness, fear of aging, fear of failure. Fear is the most basic primal instinct that we have. And, let's face it, fear sells.

Most of us are not sure what road we are on, and if we should, indeed, have taken it.

But, here we are at the beginning of a New Age, and one thing we can do is remember that we have the power to change our minds. We. Can. Start. Over. We can begin again, anew. We can stop living in fear of what may happen, that it's too late to do anything about it. Isn't it much better to live in the possibility of what may be

So, go on and get out there! Fling that cape of fear off your shoulders and wrap yourself in the sense of possibility. Seize this moment and make this new Age of Consciousness the turning point of your life! Make it a truly spectacular year, one that is filled with enormous possibilities for you!

"The more you struggle to live, the less you live. Give up the notion that you must be sure of what you are doing. Instead, surrender to what is real within you, for that alone is sure."
...Baruch Spinoza, Dutch Philosopher

Wouldn't you love to stop struggling? Wouldn't you love to be sure? You can, you know. Just go to your quiet place. That place where nobody can go to, except you. Go there. Get real...with yourself, that is. You might just find that you like what's peeking out at you from behind that corner in your heart.

Get still and surrender to that magnificent playful soul within you. Do that Happy Dance that only you can do. Hey, after all, anything's possible now. We're in a whole new wonderful era! Then walk, jump, run and start to live the life you were meant to live. Go ahead...step into that greatness and start enjoying your awesome journey!

Wiggle, wiggle, wiggle, wiggle, wiggle, wiggle, wiggle. I'm doin' the Bird Dance.

"I shall look at the world through tears. Perhaps I shall see things that, dry-eyed, I could not see."
...Nicholas Wolterstorff

We have all had times in our lives when things didn't go right, when sadness moved on us like a tide coming in. Yet, if we observe those times of seeing the world through our tears, you may notice that we were much more aware of...Every. Little. Thing. We were sensitive to everything and everyone.

And that awareness, that consciousness, allowed us to see things we wouldn't normally have seen. It enabled us to see through the moral murk. To be more understanding and less judgmental.

Well, at this most critical time in the history of mankind, that's what the Universe is asking of us now. To raise our consciousness. To co-create a new world that is based on mutual aid and co-operation. After all, it's hard to declare war on your neighbour if you don't feel it in your heart.

How do you do that? It's simple, really. When you are perhaps beginning to realize that you do not know yourself very well at all and are confronted by conflicting feelings, say to yourself "Do the right thing." Then, listen in stillness for your answer. The answer is always right there inside of you. And, you will never be steered wrong. So, let's blaze that new trail in front of us with the truth. It really is the only way forward.

"We are people who need to love, because love is the soul's life. Love is simply creation's greatest joy."
...Hafiz

Look at it this way. We've tried the fear and scarcity thing. Without a doubt, THAT'S not been effective. We certainly haven't created more abundance, less poverty, more happiness, less depression.

What we have done through living in fear and scarcity, is to create war, hunger, separation, greed, a feeling that we are never enough, we will never have enough. Does this sound like something you, in all honesty, hold to be true in your heart? Of course not. For, you are not just a body; you are a soul. And your essence is the real you.

Isn't it about time we start to restore this lost integrity, this insanity and, start establishing something good and wholesome on the Earth

Your essence is so important. Some call it your higher self. It matters not what you call it, but it is important that you get to know it. Your soul is forever. Your body, for just one lifetime.

Go forward now with confidence that you are expanding...because you are. Know that Love is the way and that you are on the right path. Now is the time to use LOVE to bring all of humanity together again. For this will activate something very powerful and, together, we will create the light necessary for everyone to become a part of it.

"Why do you stay in prison when the door is so wide open"
...Rumi

We have been getting huge doses of intense energy for some time now. Mother Earth, our Gaia-Sophia, is indeed taking steps to re-balance herself. These sparks, or solar flares (Coronal Mass Ejections) that are hitting our planet at this time are igniting us all to ponder the potion we've been drinking and consider what we are completing now...what issues and limited thinking we are ready to put behind us.

You need to make some subtle shifts so that you create a new energetic foundation. One that is in keeping with the huge gift that you are to this world!

This freedom is hard to find...like a golf ball in tall grass. But, the door is wide open. Walk through it. You'll never know what amazing things are in store for you until you do.

So, why not begin now Set a prisoner free. You might even discover that the prisoner was you.

"It may be that when we no longer know what to do, we have come to our real work, and when we no longer know which way to go, we have come to our real journey."
...Wendell Berry

It's happening. People are being led to the truth as if by accident. People who, not so long ago were totally blind to the truth, are now waking up. This is such an exciting adventure to be a part of!

For those who are waking up to what's happening out there on this beautiful planet, it's time. To dig deep down and tame that wild beast inside. To never fear the truth. Someone famous once said "The truth will set you free." It is now most important that you give your time and your effort to exploring it. It's creating a light so magnificent that it can never be extinguished!

Go on and surrender to what's real inside. Give yourself a gift. Get quiet. For you see, silence is a barricade around wisdom. Silence is a source of great strength. And, if you only knew how powerful you really are, it would...Blow. Your. Mind!

CHAPTER SIX

NO MORE COWARDLY LYIN'

"Be Yourself, because everyone else is already taken."
...Oscar Wilde

To be yourself in our cookie cutter world, where humanity is doing its best to make you like everyone else...is the most courageous act any person can do.

Please, try to remember YOU!

"There is plenty of intelligence in the world, but the courage to do things differently is in short supply."
.....Marilyn vos Savant

Sure, it's easy to go along with what everyone expects of us. It takes courage to be true to ourselves and our convictions. It takes even more courage to show that authentic self to the world.

So, stay calm and keep on keeping on. Show yourself to the world this week and do something you think you cannot do.

"Love is better than anger. Hope is better than fear. Optimism is better than despair. So, let us be loving, hopeful, and optimistic. And, we will change the world."

...Jack Layton

Leader NDP Party of Canada

(July 18, 1950 - August 22, 2011)

These were Jack Layton's final words to Canadians He died far too early. He was loved by many.

Perhaps these final words of his were bittersweet. Perhaps he discovered too late that love is better than anger. That hope is better than fear. That optimism is better than despair.

So, heed these wise words and be loving, hopeful and optimistic. And, we will change the world.

"Great spirits have always encountered violent opposition from mediocre minds."
...Albert Einstein

If we stand true to our convictions, if we have the courage to stand tall even when everyone else thinks we're nuts, what will matter is not what we got, but what we gave. What will matter is every act of integrity, compassion, courage, or sacrifice that empowered or encouraged others to live by our example.

It's not the critical, judgmental, unsupportive or misguided whose approval we seek, for they have their own issues and will eventually discover the truth for themselves. It's our own inner guidance system that we need to heed. It will never fail us. More importantly, it will give us peace. And joy!

"Youth is not a time of life - it is a state of mind,
it is a temper of the will,a quality of the
imagination,
a vigor of the emotions,
a predominance of courage over timidity,of the
appetite for adventure over love of ease.

Nobody grows old by merely living a number of
years.
People grow old only by deserting their ideals.
Years wrinkle the skin, but to give up enthusiasm
wrinkles the soul.

Worry, doubt, self-distrust, fear and despair - these
are the long,
long years that bow the head
and turn the growing spirit back to dust.

Whether they are sixteen or seventy,
there is in every being's heart
the love of wonder,
the sweet amazement at the stars
and starlike things and thoughts,
the undaunted challenge of events,
the unfailing childlike appetite
for what is to come next,
and the joy and the game of life.

You are as young as your faith,

as old as your doubt;
as young as your self-confidence,

as old as your fear,
as young as your hope,
as old as your despair.
When the wires are all down

and all the innermost core of your heart
is covered with the snows of pessimism and the ice of cynicism,
then you are grown old indeed.

But so long as your heart receives messages
of beauty, cheer, courage,
grandeur and power from the earth,
from man and from the Infinite,
so long you are young."

...Samuel Ullman

"Calm is a daily, a weekly, a monthly process, gradually changing opinions, slow eroding old barriers, quietly building new structures."
...John F. Kennedy

Yup. There is a Movement out there that is doing precisely that. Gradually changing opinions. Slowly eroding old barriers. Quietly building new structures.

The world is splitting and two pathways lay ahead. We are poised at the crossroads. We now have to consciously choose which pathway it will be. A world of love, fairness, unity, equality, abundance, and peace or the old pathway of separation, division, fear, social privilege, limitation, materialism and war.

Our Universe is evolving and we along with it. Do you know what pathway you're going down?

"Even if you're on the right track, you will get run over if you just sit there."
...Will Rogers

Taking action builds character. Taking action reveals your character.

Any dream that you have, if not followed by consistent action, however humble or small those steps may be, will result in a giant misunderstanding. The unknown is what it is.

This week, try taking action toward a goal and know that, however it turns out, you are where you are supposed to be. It is in taking the journey, that very process in and of itself, is where you really learn.

And, in so doing, you become clearer and you realize just how powerful you are! Then, wild horses couldn't stop you from taking even the humblest of baby steps, every day.

"When nothing is sure, everything is possible."
...Margaret Drabble

Once you come to realize that you have the answers inside of yourself, you can stop searching outside of yourself.

It isn't so much about overcoming fear, as it is about not settling for less. Sometimes, when you have a sense of uncertainty, feelings of discomfort, or a twinge of unhappiness, that's when the seeds of great accomplishment are sown.

Think highly of yourself. Because no matter how high that is, it will still be an underestimate of how great you really are.

**"Bad news is...Time flies. Good news is...You're the Pilot."
...Michael Altshuler**

Yep. The last year flew by in the wink of an eye. There is a whole new list of possibilities for You! How are you going to navigate your life?

Spend your time wisely. Be the overseer of your own thoughts throughout the day.

Are your thoughts investing your energy where it isn't useful Perhaps there is a deeper hunger there for personal growth, acceptance by others or, emotional closeness...

Take a Quantum Leap for yourself. Stop draining your brain. Retrain it instead. Be consciously aware that a moment's thought can help you see the true nature of what you may be lusting after.

Today, try to keep your thoughts in the present moment. Take a magic carpet ride, fly to the moon, dance in daisies and use your imagination to create a wonderful year for Your Self!

"Success is not the key to happiness. Happiness is the key to success. If you love what you are doing, you will be successful."
...Albert Schweitzer

When you have a vision for your life, you have a passion and joy that cannot be described. And in trying to create that vision, any obstacles will be a blur because you are so committed to following through that you can't imagine anything stopping you.

The key is to work harder on yourself than you do your job. Think as only you can think. Which will lead to feelings only you can feel. Feelings that in turn, create connections, move mountains, and open up worlds you can't even dream of.

When you work on yourself, the irony is that it isn't what you've created that stands out. What impresses the marketplace is your determination and persistence to keep at something even when the outcome is not assured. That you hold steadfast to the success of your vision and move with it is what makes you more valuable to the world at large. That is what is so admired. Because it is so rare.
Follow your heart. Your life will grow in leaps and bounds.

"Go out on a limb, that's where the best fruit is."
... Mark Twain

It takes a lot to knock over a tree with deep roots. It's the same with people. Your roots help to support you and nourish you and help you stand erect when a strong wind blows your way. It's up to you to grow strong, powerful, healthy roots. Your family, your friends, your community will all help you do this.

And if you do, it's much easier to venture out onto that limb because even if a strong gust comes along, you may bow, you may bend, but you won't break. Besides, what's a little shakeup when the limb is where all the yummy fruit is anyway!

"And the day came when the risk to remain tight in a bud was more painful than the risk it took to blossom."
...Anais Nin

In the end, what will matter will be what you have built, not what you have bought. What will matter is what you gave, not what you got. What will matter is your character not your proficiency. What will matter is the unflinching choice to make a stand for yourself and act with courage, in spite of consequences. It takes courage to shine. And this is good.

Ride on, brave heart.

"Surround yourself with the dreamers and the doers, the believers and the thinkers, but most of all surround yourself with those who see the greatness within you, even when you don't see it yourself."
...Edmund Lee

Ahhh...There's magic in believing. Especially at these crossroads of time where people are yearning to awaken and find the truth about themselves, to determine what talents and gifts they have been blessed with, to discover the divinity and magic that is within them. These people who see that potential in you are priceless! Money can't buy that kind of support!

You know what's kinda wild These same people are the ones who encourage you to take that next step, to keep climbing that mountain even when each step is a tough go, each step is a challenge. Even when the higher you go, the harder it gets because you are tired. And sore from working so hard.

But, here's the beautiful thing...as you keep taking those baby steps, the air becomes clearer, the view magnificent.

And, Bazinga! You finally see the magic of yourself.

"Experience is both the most difficult and the best teacher because it gives you the exam first, and the lesson second."
...Unknown

What has experience taught us in this changing world? Well, that it's really okay to make mistakes. Yup. We all make 'em. We all survive 'em. And, hopefully we all learn from them.

Yet, it's really counter-intuitive to what we've all be taught. In this linear-thinking world that we grew up in, we have learned that we're supposed to get it right the first time...that it's not alright to make mistakes. And, if we do, we're inept, or incompetent, or just plain stupid!

But, here's an amazing insight. The leaders that are rising to the top these days don't have all the answers. They just ask the right questions.

So, your mission this week, if you choose to accept it, is to go out there and jump into life with both feet! If you don't, you may indeed escape the missteps, or, you may self-destruct. But, most importantly, you'll miss the rush and the mind-blowing thrill of new discoveries. About yourself. Our world. Our life.

Just JUMP! Take that exam first! The lessons you will learn Priceless.

"We all walk in the dark and each of us must learn to turn on his or her own light."
...Earl Nightingale

There is magic in the air. We are on very fertile ground full of pure possibility. This is the energy we have been waiting for. This is the energy we will be creating from, and it all begins with us. Can you feel it?

You can, if you get quiet enough. If you sit still, you can feel that pulsing from within. It's what is bringing balance to both the heart and the mind but is giving the heart a much bigger voice. It's not a thought and it's not a feeling but, rather, something much deeper and more profound.

So, whatever you desire is contained in this energy. Whatever you have the courage to imagine is within this energy. Look it straight in the face. Tune in to it. This is the stuff that will create our new world. And, this is just the tipping point, the start of a wonderful spiral upward.

So, now's the time to step out of the darkness. It's time to turn on your light, run into the sunshine and embrace your new playground!

"If everybody is thinking alike, somebody isn't thinking."
...Henry Ford

We have been immersed in a culture that gets us to do what it wants us to do. It's produced a cookie cutter society. Where we do the things and are the people who we've been told to be. And, let's face it, when you put fences around people...you get sheep.

It's about time we change that, don't you think

All we have to do is tear down our fences, talk with our neighbours once again. We need to get rid of our TVs, quit eating genetically modified foods, see that money means nothing in the grand scheme of things. We need to stop getting others to do our thinking for us. We do realize that our credit cards don't love us back don't we

We all need to get to that place of vulnerability. Because vulnerability is the birthplace of innovation, of creativity, and of CHANGE. It is also the most accurate measurement of COURAGE. For it takes courage to trust yourself and open to new possibilities for your future. Of letting go of what people say you are, to be who YOU are.

And, another word for courage It's HEART. It all starts there. And I'll let you in on a secret. Your heart knows what to do...

"'You must try to forget all you have learned,' said the old man. 'You must begin to dream. From this time on you must shut your ears to the roaring of the voices.'"
...Sherwood Anderson
Author of Winesburg, Ohio

These days there are a ton of roaring voices. Everywhere. All over the world. Telling us we must do this, or we are duty-bound to do that...

But, what we really need to do, what we must discover for ourselves, is that our safety and our security comes from within us. For, when we shut off the world and get quiet, get really still...no one can affect us in negative ways because we are in balance inside. By making choices from the heart, we can begin this journey. But you already know this.

Remembering is part of the work you are here on earth to do. The very fact that you have forgotten what happened to you before you came to this earth plane is why it takes so much courage.

You have chosen to be on earth at this most critical time in history for a very important reason. And, you have work to do. You just don't remember. But, if you take the time to do this work, it can give you the courage to work through those daunting challenges and trust the ancient wisdom inside each and every one of you. You carry this information in your soul. All you have to do is remember.

Go ahead and clear out the parasites in your mind. Fall back in love with the beauty on this planet and with your life. As you tune out the noise and get quiet with yourself, remember how brave you are. Honour yourself. Help others to awaken. And, then let us all come together in the name of LOVE.

"You didn't come into this world. You came out of it, like a wave from the ocean. You are not a stranger here."
...Alan Watts

The fact that we came here and lost all memory of what happened to us before we were born is one of the many reasons that it takes so much courage to be here. This is also why, when you start to question your reason for being here, it so often feels like a remembering ...because it is.

It is not a coincidence that you are Here. Now. Start remembering who YOU are. You can begin by remembering that we are all connected. It's IMPORTANT work. It's POWERFUL work.

Go out there and begin. Begin to find your way home.

CHAPTER SEVEN

HOPELESSLY DEVOTED TO ME

"Neither a lofty degree of intelligence, nor imagination, nor both together go to the making of genius. Love, love, love...that is the soul of genius."
...Mozart

The world is wobbling at a rapid rate at this point in history and you may be moving through periods of intense fear, loss, and uncertainty; you may feel that these emotions make you feel off balance, almost as if you are spinning at a different rate than the planet. Know this, and look to these emotions as your teacher. Allow them to free you.If there ever was a time to tune in and listen to your heart, it is now!

Feel your heart beating. Start with you. Just breathe. There are treasures within your own heart! Feel your heart beating. Remember that you are alive, you are in a body, and you live on this planet.

Just for this week, try to get in closer touch with your own personal rhythms, see your patterns and learn from them. Look within and love yourself first.

"We don't read and write poetry because it's cute. We read and write poetry because we are members of the human race. And the human race is filled with passion. And, medicine, law, business, engineering, these are noble pursuits and necessary to sustain life. But, poetry, beauty, romance, love, these are what we stay alive for." ...from the movie Dead Poets Society

Originally, I had allowed this quote to stand on its own because it was so powerful.

Since the death of Robin Williams, I felt he should be mentioned as he was the professor in this movie trying to instill passion into his young protégés. As brilliant and funny as he was, Robin Williams was a humanitarian first. He reflected his TRUTH in this portrayal in the film.

I honour Robin Williams here. He was a beautiful soul who gave much love and laughter to this planet. But no matter how hard he tried, he could not seem to find the love that was there all the time…hidden deep down inside of himself.

May he find the peace that evaded him on this earth plane.

"To love and win is the best thing. To love and lose, the next best."
...William M. Thackery

Loving and winning is wonderful!

Sometimes though, the most helpful thing you could do for someone is to let them go so they could learn stuff at their own pace. It's also one of the most helpful things you can do for yourself.

Because, just around the corner of change, something better is being created just for you! Something better than it's ever been before.

Live, love, laugh...empower, dance, and free them all...

"Do you want me to tell you something really subversive? Love is everything it's cracked up to be. That's why people are so cynical about it....It really is worth fighting for, being brave for, risking everything for. And the trouble is if you don't risk anything, you risk even more."
...Erica Jong

Aaahhh Love. What a little word for such a huge concept. When you glance at two people in love, you feel almost like an intruder yet, you cannot seem to peel your eyes away from them because they emanate such warmth that you just want to be a part of that embrace. It's almost as if you can intuitively see that connection.

Love is what deeply inspires you, what fills you with a burning passion. When it gets right down to it, love is everything. Allow yourself to open your heart. Why? Because you're worth it.

"The greatest problem in the world is not hunger of the stomach, but hunger of the heart."
...Mother Teresa

There are more telephones...but less communication, more communication...but less connection, more connection...but less attachment.

Some people suffer intolerable loneliness today. Do you ever feel this way? It is simply your heart sending you a message to connect. Connect with another soul.

In your loneliness, you have forgotten that we are all connected. You need only to reach out to another human being with an offer to connect. That connection may gift you with a piece of the puzzle in the search for yourself. Let's face it, we are all searching for ourselves. Why not make it easier and stop hiding from ourselves? In the words of Bruce Springsteen, "Everybody needs a place to rest, everybody wants to have a home. Don't make no difference what nobody says, ain't nobody like to be alone. Everybody's got a hungry heart..." Go on now. Reach out and touch someone.

"The earth does not belong to human beings; human beings belong to the earth."
...Chief Seattle

Did you do anything special in honour of Earth Day? She is Gaia-Sophia after all, the mother who birthed us. We grew from her womb.

Although technology has brought us many wonderful blessings, it has also disconnected us from nature and from each other. We have, inadvertently, cut ourselves off from our roots and we need to reclaim our connection to the earth. We cannot deny the roots of our past.

We all need to honour and reconnect to the sacredness, the wisdom, within this planet.We cannot have harmony and balance in ourselves if we neglect our Earth's natural rhythms and cycles. The more attuned we are to our senses, our bodies, and our planet, the more grounded, present, and powerful we can be.

Tap into your roots and you will soon find nourishment for your body and stimulation for your spirit. The profound peace you feel when you are in the mountains or looking up at a starry night...this is the food for your soul. This is a source that we share with all of humanity. This is Love. Enjoy it. Embrace it.

"The most beautiful and profound emotion we can experience is the sensation of the mystical. It is the power of all true science."
...Albert Einstein

The more I discover things Albert Einstein said, the more I am convinced he was just as much a philosopher as he was a physicist.

Love can be like the mystical. If you have ever experienced this profound emotion, you can know with absolute certainty that it came from the wisdom of the Universe. And, that's the problem with love. You only know when you've found it because it "just feels right" or you feel that they "just get me." There are no adequate words.

Today, this week, if there is a special someone whom you've shared this mystical sensation with...run, don't walk, to embrace them! Maybe it's not always about trying to fix something broken. Maybe it's about starting over and creating something better.

You see, if you feel what you feel about that person, it's because you are being drawn by a force that needs to be honoured. Trust it.

"As we heal ourselves, we heal the world." ...Louise Hay

When life throws you a challenge, or a major setback, or a heartache, it is also extending you a gift. A gift to heal.

We are our own best healers. We know ourselves best, after all! But how do you start to heal yourself

You tune into your body. Your body, by far, is the most sensitive barometer of your inner world. When you start to pay attention to the signals your body gives you, you learn to trust yourself more.

As you learn to look after yourself, and be gentle with yourself, and let go of those resistant negative thoughts, you begin to see the unlimited, mind-blowing possibilities that are there...right at your fingertips. And, you will start to see how powerful you really are.

"By going out of your mind, you come to your senses. When you come out of the conditioned, limited, and unaware mind, the centre of gravity naturally shifts to the heart."
...Alan Watts

Strengthening your mind is like strengthening your body. It takes time. Exercising your body takes practice, persistence and commitment to regular workouts. Exercising your mind requires exactly the same thing.

As with a healthy body, where your centre of gravity shifts to a vigorous, vibrant state, a healthy mind shifts exactly the same way.

"If you don't build your dream, someone will hire you to build theirs."
...Unknown

This is not a time of doom and gloom. It's a time of great joy and celebration as the earth re-balances herself and prepares for the shift into this new age that we are entering. Why not make it a time to re-balance yourself?

Why not start by getting back in touch with nature? Nature has such a simplicity and we can gain much from her. Nature will help guide you in building a dream for yourself. For, when you recognize your truth, you'll feel it in your heart. And, when you follow your heart, a lot of those rules that people think are necessary, aren't...because you're doing things from love.

Your energy goes to whatever you believe in. If you believe in yourself and your own inner wisdom, that energy comes to you. And, it's that energy we use to activate all the abilities within us.

So, "let's rock on down to Electric Avenue and let the energy take you higher..." wiggle, wiggle, wiggle, wiggle, wiggle.

"For one moment our lives met, our souls touched."
...Oscar Wilde

You are where you are supposed to be. Now. At this moment in history. At this moment in time. People come and go in your life for reasons that are sometimes unknown to you. Sometimes they come as unanswered prayers. Sometimes they come as gifts all wrapped up in different packaging.

There is a difference between who you love, who you settle with, and who you're meant for. There's a difference between the love of a mother for her child, the love of a sister for her brother, and the love of your life. But, this much I know...

There are people you meet in life that make everything seem magical. Cherish them. Honour them. For they will forever be in your soul.

"Oh, pride and competition cannot fill these empty arms, and the work I put between us, you know it doesn't keep me warm..."
...Don Henley,
The End of the Innocence

Why is it that we get so caught up in the day-to-day drudgery of getting our job done? To become better than the other guy? Why do we hide how we really feel? How come we continue with bitter feuds years, even decades, after the original conflict is over? Honestly...Who does it really hurt other than our own self?

Pride. Competition. These are learned behaviours. Limiting beliefs. What if the struggle we've been taught is natural, turns out to be the most unnatural thing we could be doing?

Passion, on the other hand, is such a primal human trait. We all know what it is, what it feels like. Whether it's passion for another person, a place, or an activity, passion is what propels us forward. It's what allows us to have greater life experiences. And, in the end, it's what teaches us more about ourselves, and what we can do.

Opt for passion. Instead of pride. Instead of competition. Catch the light....and watch the miracles begin to happen.

"Even after all this time the Sun never says to the Earth, 'You owe me.' Look what happens with a love like that. It lights up the whole sky."
... Hafiz

The possibility of stepping into a higher plane is real. It doesn't require that you give up everything you hold dear. It simply asks that you change your ideas about what is possible.

We are all experiencing Mother Earth, Gaia-Sophia, rebalancing herself. And, just as our earth is now vibrating at higher levels, our bodies are adapting and changing to those higher frequencies as well.

Be gentle with yourself. Be kind to yourself. Love yourself first and remember the Golden Rule. For you see...Love really does conquer all.

"There will be a time when you believe everything is finished. That will be the beginning."
...Louis L'Amour

According to the Mayan Calendar, the end of time was on December 21st,. But, just as we observe the end of a caterpillar's life, it is also when we see the beginning of a butterfly's.

So, at this special time when family and loved ones are closest in mind and heart, a time when you have a tenderness for the past, and a hope for the future, please take this time to feel that you are being smiled upon and held ever so gently because you are precious and rare.

And, like the plain caterpillar who becomes a beautiful butterfly, may your soul become restored and nourished and may you experience an anticipation of the breathtakingly spectacular beauty unfolding around you.

May the peace, happiness and joy of all seasons embrace you....and remember, keep shining, this world needs your warmth.

"When the power of love overcomes the love of power, the world will know peace."
...Jimi Hendrix

What if this whole evolutionary journey that we are now on is to just have a willingness and be open to whatever it is that is coming in? What if knowing that kind of thing doesn't really matter at all?

The truth is, the desire "to know" is born from a fear of the unknown. The future is yours to love. It's your choice. And, it won't be defined by your past.

So, it's now time to take a walk in the dark without a light. To remember what it means to "feel" your way. You all know those days of playing hide and seek in the dark The thrill of finding something or someone you weren't expecting

Well...Fasten your seatbelts. You're in for a wild ride! Yee Haw!

As the energies on this planet become more intense, (in a good way) and time is spinning faster and faster, all that knowledge that you have, will get peeled back. And, your soul, that part of you that holds and protects your wisdom, will know that love is really the only way home. You are beginning to understand the importance of love. For you see, LOVE survives all.

"The greatest good you can do for another is not just to share your riches, but to reveal to him, his own."
...Benjamin Disraeli

As we move into this new world that is evolving every day around us, do you feel as if you're in a holding pattern You know, that we are leaving old paradigms behind...but you're not sure where we are headed

You are not alone! The key lies in realizing the power of the heart. And its innate intelligence – knowing, NOT thinking. And, let's face it, there are more nerves going from the heart to the brain than coming the other way.

The fact is, if the heart and the brain and the central nervous system are in harmony, then you go into a completely different, and much, much higher level of consciousness and awareness.

And, the fabric that holds all this together Compassion. So, go out and use yours this week. Reveal to someone how GREAT they truly are.

When I think of all the people who have enriched my life with their unique gifts, I realize, indeed, how very wealthy I am.

"Be the person your dog thinks you are."
...Unknown

Oh, to love unconditionally. That's what your dog does every single time you step through that front door. Smiling. Wagging its tail. Glad to have you home.

It's like that movie classic, "Avatar," when the girl from Pandora looks into Jake's eyes and says, "I SEE YOU." And means, I REALLY see who you are. That moment brought tears to millions of eyes when they saw that scene...even people who are not awake were moved by that moment. Why? Because everybody wants to be seen, wants to be recognized, acknowledged.

Your dog sees who you REALLY are. Now go out, and shine to the planet, the gift that you are to this world.

"Character cannot be developed in ease and quiet. Only through experience of trial and suffering can the soul be strengthened, ambition inspired, and success achieved."
...Helen Keller

As I come in exhausted after a day of doing my part to save our planet, these words swirl around in my head.

When I just can't seem to find the strength to go it another day, to face one more cause, to rally up the energy to exert one last ounce of energy, when I fumble and grasp because everyone and everything around me is in doubt, these words ring in my ears. And, I know that my work is far from over.

I believe each of us has a truth that rumbles within us. Something that gives us the reason for being. We are all here at this point in time for a reason. And, we have all this spiritual energy that has brought love to a place that needs it the most. The HERE and NOW.

So, if you have come through a transformation of sorts...a time when, on some days you could barely get out of bed, a time when your body has been so filled with tension that it refuses to move any more, it may have shown you what is important, what really matters. Perhaps you have seen other people on the same path.

Seen their joys and their struggles. And, then you know you are not alone.

You see, the entire world is starting to unite. Yes, oh yes, people have had enough. The old system is at an end. Anyone who is awake, knows that. And, know this. All you need is love. Love is the answer. Know this, too...while you're out there trying to make a difference...you ARE the difference.

"When you live on a round planet there is no choosing sides."
...Dr. Wayne Dyer

Years ago astronauts went up into space and took photos of this planet we all share. To this day when we see these photos, it evokes in us a sense of reverence, a sense of awe...

For when those astronauts looked back to Earth from way up there in outer space, they saw no division lines. They didn't see the U.S. or Canada. They didn't see India, or China, or Russia. What they saw was one whole planet....what they saw was that we are all connected.

So, as we move into The Age of Consciousness, the gifts we've developed as children...you know, those gifts of technology, computers, agriculture etc. well, we now need to apply them to our true purpose.

There is a lot of healing that must be done, to the environment, to the economy, to the community, to us. And, it's almost impossible really. Almost.

There are no sides. We are now...everyone on this planet... in the business of creating a miracle here on earth. When we all come together and realize the importance of love, we will rescue our planet.

What it gets down to, really, is whether we love each other enough to save the world. Think with your heart. Feel with your mind. It's time for us all to awaken and do the right thing. It's "one small step for man. One giant leap for mankind."

"Magic's just science that we don't understand yet."
...Arthur C. Clarke

Take the science of your heart. The heart is not a squishy, sentimental object. Did you know that it's a high performance state?

Heart intelligence is highly intelligent. It is very aware. Not only that, it's useful in relationships, in athletics, in business. Go figure.

Wherever you go, when you take your heart along, you change your physiological and psychological states. Yes, oh yes, you do! And, you can apply the benefits...reducing the score of a game, or higher productivity at work.

It all involves the heart. And that's where science makes the bridge.

It's simple, really. Your brain is electrical, your heart is magnetic. And there's way more intelligence going from the heart to the brain than the other way around.

Use your heart to guide you. Practice. Use this tool until it is a natural expression of who you are...as natural as eating with a fork or driving a car. It will take you to a place inside yourself where you can be more than you usually are...beyond mediocrity.

Come on. You can do this! Everybody's got a hungry heart... Guaranteed you will start to see some magic of your own!

"What the caterpillar calls the end of the world, the master calls the butterfly."
...Chuang Tse

There is this great secret that everyone knows except us, in the West. Almost every other culture that we go to from the monasteries in Egypt and India, to little villages in the Andes mountains, to the Mayans...they all know that there is this experience that we can have inside of our bodies that affects our world in some way.

There is something we can do in our lives that not only influences our body, and those of other people around us, but literally influences the physical reality of our world. And, that changes everything that we, in the West, believe about ourselves.

We have the opportunity to influence that field in ways that we are only beginning to understand. It's done through the heart. It is not a thinking process.

Our thoughts are electrical. Our hearts are magnetic. So, when we have feelings in our hearts, we are changing the field that connects the stuff everything is made of and we are literally altering our physical reality in ways that sound miraculous in Western science.

We're just now beginning to understand that human emotion and feeling and belief are, at their most basic form, a language, a non-verbal language that is extremely powerful.

It's time for us to be very very aware of what it is that we truly hold in our hearts as it becomes the truth that is our world.

To survive this time in history, we've got to rewrite ourselves back into the equation. Your heart has the wisdom. Your mind has the stories. Now's the time to transition into that beautiful butterfly. Bottom line....You gotta have heart.

"Only from the heart can you touch the sky."
...Rumi

Simple. And yet, for centuries we have tossed that painless concept aside. For what War Poverty Greed Corruption And, has it worked

In a word...No. The lesson we can take from all of this is that it, heartbreakingly, didn't work.

We all know that now, in hindsight, and we are shifting inside. Because of that...our outer world follows and shifts, as well. The foundation of life is now morphing into something new and stronger.

Slowly, but surely, we are coming to the realization that we all live in this realm of consciousness that is reflecting back to us not what we think in our minds, but what we feel in our hearts.

The most powerful weapon on earth is not war, nor guns nor even our minds...it's the human soul on fire. Use that weapon. Then, and only then, will we soar.

"We are each of us angels with only one wing, and we can only fly by embracing one-another."
...Luciano de Crescenzo

The holidays are a magical time of year. While some people get grumpy, it's true, most others have feelings of good will toward all.

And, there's fairy dust filled with laughter floating among those of us who are willing to see the magic of life. It really does rub off on you just by close proximity.

May all your holidays be warm and wonderful with your family and friends...ones filled with laughter and good times, grace and awe at this special time and all year long. May you all remember too, the reason for the season.

"You may say I'm a dreamer. But I'm not the only one. I hope one day you'll join us. And the world will live as one."
...John Lennon

Prophetic words by a prophet of our time.

You can join us by listening to the whispers of your heart. By hearing the flutter of feathers in your soul.

Start living from your heart centre. Let that brain in your heart move you in the right direction. Let all that you do be with peace and love in your heart. And, then watch our evolution soar!

Imagine.

Namaste.

CHAPTER EIGHT

LETTING GO TO RECEIVE

"Only the brave know how to forgive. A coward never forgives; it is not in his nature."
...Laurence Stern

Forgiveness is huge! Forgiveness is the way! Forgiveness is the answer to almost everything! It is a great healer. It can heal your heart, your mind, your body, and your life!

As resentment is the opposite of forgiveness, you only end up harming yourself. It is like taking poison and expecting someone else to die.

Forgiveness is not forgetting. It is not denying what happened or your feelings about it. Forgiveness is not excusing the other person of his or her actions. Forgiveness is unconditional. Forgiveness is something you do for yourself.

Who do you have to forgive today?

"All that is required for evil to triumph, is for good men to do nothing."
...Edmund Burke

The Shift is here. Now. It's all about how you transition into this new way that's most important. And, it really comes down to how you think about yourself and your world around you.

Take judgement, for instance. Did you know that the biggest judgement is within us? Why not release that judgement and allow yourself to be a big, bright, beautiful being that you are?

Here's an analogy. You're walking down the grocery aisle and you see wonderful strawberries, and you think, "Yum." Then you see apples and cantaloupes...the same thing... "yummy." Then you happen to see pumpernickel and you go, "Yuck." You take it a step further and think to yourself, "Pumpernickel should not even be here!" Now you are starting to judge. We do it all the time. Without awareness.

Why not simply put your energy on what you love? Continue down that aisle...see the pumpernickel, and then go on to see those succulent peaches...and mangoes...See the pumpernickel but don't allow yourself to be drawn into a judgement of that item.

You can start by noticing things as insignificant as that. You will soon come to realize that a little light pushes away a lot of darkness. The way I see it....doing a little somethin' somethin' is better than doing a whole lot of nothin'.

"Weakness of attitude becomes weakness of character."
...Albert Einstein

How many times have we all heard, "I'll be happy when...I get that new promotion, that new car, that new relationship" How many times does our anger become the go-to emotion?

These attitudes are habits that we have created for ourselves that are really not feeding us well. Anger and excuses do not enhance character, at all. These emotions detract from it and are an obstacle to growth.

For, what's really happening when you resort to excuses or anger, is that something deep inside of you is demanding acknowledgement and attention.

Next time anger or excuses rear their ugly heads, start to take notice. You may be able to see a pattern. A trigger perhaps. Anger can be a powerful ally which contains a huge amount of energy and, if harnessed in the right way, can create change in the world.

So, let these poor attitudes be cathartic for you....a cleansing of your emotional system. And, then just watch the transformation that starts to work in your life!

"Holding on to anger is like grasping a hot coal with the intent of throwing it at someone else; you are the one who gets burned."
...Buddha

Forgiveness is so huge. Do you wanna know a secret? It really is the key to almost everything.

We all carry around a past with us every day. And, sometimes that past can still be quite active and rear its ugly head as resentment, judgement, guilt, shame and so on. With that past, comes a negative energy that we are, unknowingly, carrying around with us. It blocks the flow of good energy. So, if we truly want to be happy, we must release all of our negative energy.

Forgiveness is a perfect way to do this. It is also a great healer. It can heal your heart, your mind, your body, and your soul by releasing the destructive energy of anger and resentment from your consciousness. Forgiveness dissolves resentment. It's a process, a life-time habit more than it is a one-time action. Forgiveness is something you do for yourself.

Let's get rid of some emotional baggage this week and forgive someone! Psssst...it really is the key to everything.

"An eye for an eye will only make everyone blind." ...Gandhi

Today and every Memorial Day, is a day to remember. A day to give thanks to those who gave their lives for us in the name of their country.

To remember...Your life is a gift and not a given right. To remember...that freedom is precious, my friends. And, to remember, really remember, that the only way forward is in peace and not war. Even the thought of that brings forth a sense of serenity within us.

We now know that war does not work. Have you ever noticed anything containing the word "war" be successful War on Drugs. War on Cancer. War on Poverty. War on Terrorism.

No. Now is the time for us to remember. Remember who we are. Trust the ancient wisdom that we carry inside of us. Those fallen soldiers would want that. Those fallen soldiers are calling from their graves for us to remember.

Let us give honour and give recognition to our brave warriors by doing this and coming together in peace and in love. For, our Light will revive the entire world.

CHAPTER NINE

STILL WATERS RUN DEEP

"Four Thousand volumes of metaphysics will not teach us what the soul is."
...Voltaire

Only you can discover that for yourself. Learning how to become calm is a good start, for we all need our own quiet place. The funny thing is, the quieter you become, the more you can hear.

Practice being calm every day and before long, you will start to hear your soul awaken. What joy!

"The more tranquil a man becomes, the greater is his success, his influence, his power for good. Calmness of mind is one of the beautiful jewels of wisdom."
...James Allen

People are suffering every day all over this planet, be it from stress, depression, mental illness.

When we realize that it's not about "doing-ness," it's about "being-ness"...that's when a sense of quiet will enter our soul and embed itself in our spirit.

Instead of listening to that monkey mind of yours, try to just "be" with who you are this week. Try to recapture your personal power and embrace yourself! You are unique. You are powerful. You are a gift to this world.

"War does not determine who is right – only who is left."
...Bertrand Russell

War does not work. It does make a lot of money for certain groups of people....

Think about it. War against crime. War against terrorism. War against drugs. War against cancer. War against poverty. Have you ever won these battles It is all condemned to failure. Why? Because it's war. And, in the bigger picture, war on the world stage is only because humanity has been at war with itself. You can stop this. Now.

When you go to your quiet place, you will come to your senses. When you get out of your head, your centre of gravity will gently and automatically shift to your heart. There is no one who does not want peace.

Everywhere you go today, go in peace. Get out of your head. Remember. Know in your heart...war does not work.

"If you do not go within....you simply go without." ...Victor Frankl

Honestly. This planet is changing right before your very eyes. This transformation can leave you feeling confused, spinning out of control, and scared. You may look to the environment, to material things, to other people for reassurance. All the while, the place you need to look for solace and comfort and happiness has been there, waiting for you patiently.

To find what you need, you must go within. Every....single...time... You need to start accessing a part of your brain that has been dormant for centuries...the archaic brain. You see, you have all the wisdom of the Universe right inside of you. If accessed, you will instinctively act in integrity, and be authentic, not only to everyone you connect with, but, most importantly, to yourself! Look within.

"Silence. All human unhappiness comes from not knowing how to stay quietly in a room."
...Blaise Pascal (1623-1662)

Everybody needs their own quiet place. It starts with you. You need only one thing. Self-trust. An authentic relationship begins with a Divine relationship with your spirit, with your sacred self.

This week, try by letting go of that mind chatter, that monkey mind. Forget those stories in your head that pretend to be you. Get rid of that clutter because, when you live from a place of truth, it will bring you peace. Peace brings happiness. Everybody needs their own quiet place.

"The most important thing in communication is hearing what isn't said."
...Peter Drucker

We do it every day. Talk to people. Have conversations. But to really communicate...that is an art because it takes talent and skill. And silence is one of the great arts of communication.

Have you ever felt so comfortable with someone that you felt no need to speak No awkward moments. You just sat in silence together.

Sometimes more can be said in silence than can ever be said with words. Start listening to the silence this week and you just might be amazed by what you hear.

"Thinking is the hardest work there is which is the probable reason why so few people engage in it." ...Henry Ford

Why is it we have more knowledge these days, yet less wisdom, more degrees, but less common sense, more abundance, yet less happiness, more medicine, yet less wellness?

You have to work hard to get your thinking clear and clean. However, most people's thinking is involuntary, and automatic, and repetitive. In essence, you don't think. Thinking happens to you. The voice in your head has a mind of its own, and most people live in the indulgence of that voice.

Next time you come up against a challenge or a struggle, with either yourself or others, stop. Check in with yourself. Perhaps those disappointments are merely a manifestation of what's going on within your own thinking. A story you've told yourself.

Once you get your thinking crystal clear, the rest then, becomes simple.

"Trust the one who can see these three things in you: Sorrow behind your smile, love behind your anger, and meaning behind your silence."
...Deejay Nismo

Huge. As you leap into a new beginning for "You," most of all, trust yourself. Remember, the reason wise souls enjoy spending time alone is because they never really are.

"Peace. It does not mean to be in a place where there is no noise, trouble or hard work. It means to be in the midst of those things and still be calm in your heart."
...Unknown

The path of peace flows like a river. It resists nothing. And because of this, it wins before it even begins. To be at peace can't be beaten because no one is fighting against anyone, only themselves.

In the end, if you conquer yourself, you will conquer this Universe.

"Happiness is a butterfly, which when pursued, is always just beyond your grasp, but which, if you sit down quietly, may alight upon you."
...Nathaniel Hawthorne

How many times have you said to yourself, "I'll be happy WHEN...I get that new car, new job, new house, new relationship." Why? Why are you postponing your happiness? It is not in the future. Happiness is in the present moment.

Just go to the park and watch children play. They are living in the present moment. And, they are full of innocence, joy, playfulness, sweetness, love. Without even thinking about it!

The next time you feel guilty about being happy, or feel you don't deserve to be happy...STOP. Sit down quietly and make a good choice for yourself. It is your birthright to be happy.

"You are here to allow the divine purpose of the Universe to unfold. That is how important you are."
...Eckhart Tolle

Your soul chose to be here at this time in history. You have very important things to do. From the unknown comes the creativity and inventiveness that you need to help you succeed.

That and the ability to trust the silence...feel the quiet...embrace the calm. For, it's in the silence between your thoughts, that great messages are received, insights gained, and wisdom bestowed.

Believe. YOU are that powerful.

"Perhaps the most important thing we bring to another person is the silence in us, not the sort of silence that is filled with unspoken criticism or hard withdrawal. The sort of silence that is a place of refuge, of rest, of acceptance of someone as they are.

We are all hungry for this silence. It is hard to find.

In its presence, we can remember something beyond the moment, strength on which to build a life.

Silence is a place of great power and healing."

...Rachel Naomi Remen

"You'd give anything to silence, those voices ringing in your head. You thought you could find happiness, just over that green hill. You thought that you'd be satisfied, but you never will....Learn to be still."

...Don Henley
The Eagles

It's a jungle out there. Chances are that it's also a jungle inside your head. Jaws roaring, fangs snapping, voices niggling. Running on and on and on. Eventually, all that running leads you to running smack into yourself.

Why not get quiet, I mean really quiet, and sit with Your Self? Silence is a place of great power and healing. Stillness is a fence around wisdom. For you see the voice that whispers is every bit as important as the voice that shouts. But you have to get quiet to be able to hear it. And, to the mind that becomes still...the whole universe surrenders.

"I discovered I scream the same way whether I'm about to be devoured by a Great White Shark or if a piece of seaweed touches my foot."
...Axel Rose

Lately I've been feeling exhausted, bored, over-stimulated, fat and have a really weird feeling of being disconnected.

So, I've figured out that if I take the time to sit in stillness and in quiet, to let go of all that crap that natters away in my head 24/7, I soon discover that perhaps that air guitar rendition of "Born in the U.S.A." that I mentally play in my head is not really necessary when it's time to be still.

Instead of a commentary that goes something like this: "I forgot to pick up toothpaste. How sloppy am I? My foot's itchy. When will my nose stopping running like a faucet?" Then, a chorus of "I Heard It Through the Grapevine," and back to "How am I gonna remember to get that toothpaste?" I begin to notice that when I take the time to shut the noise out of my chattering brain, I become noticeably less distracted the next time.

And, there is more clarity. More energy. It's like I HAVE taken that vacation to the sunny south. I feel refreshed. This is the power of taking a calm moment for YOU!

"Young souls look to secrets, rights and rituals. Mature souls look to science, math and evidence. Old souls look within. Look within."
...Mike Dooley

It is all there inside of you. In that quiet place where most people fear to tread. But it's there. All the knowledge, and all the wisdom you will ever need.

We were all born with the potential to do anything we applied ourselves to. We were all born with the ability to heal ourselves. We seemed to have lost that talent about 13,000 years ago when we began to live in our brains and forgot about our hearts.

But, it's all there in our memory, waiting for us to remember. All we have to do is to start leaving the brain and all the chatter that goes on there, and moving back into the heart and living there. Actually seeing with the eyes of your heart, and not the brain, and living there. We know exactly how to do this. It's a memory and it will come back at the right moment.

You can start practicing by sitting in stillness for five minutes a day. The key is to listen to the silence in between the thoughts because this activates dormant connections to your soul's consciousness. Then watch the magic that begins to happen!

"A mind is like a parachute. It doesn't work if it's not open."
...Frank Zappa

In order for your brain to be open, you must first accept that the Universe is biased in the favour of Love, Peace, and Forgiveness. For, if you practice this within yourself, it has a collective, energetic effect on business.

Supporting data is mind-blowing. Think about this: If enough people feel anger, fear, stress and pain, then disasters are more likely to occur. Think back to the event of April 15th, 2013. For Americans, this is the tax deadline. Lots of stress in people. What happened then? The Boston Marathon Bombing.

Positive emotions protect us from these disasters. We must develop an awareness of keeping those negative emotions and thoughts out of our minds because these thoughts ultimately lower our "defense shields."

And, as Deepak Chopra has said, when people tell him that they don't believe in meditation, his response is that "they must not believe in the brain, because four decades of brain research have proven that the brain is transformed by meditation." He then goes on to say that "newer evidence suggests that genetic output also improves with meditation. That is, the right genes get switched on and the wrong ones get switched off." Wow. Really.

Perhaps you can try to open your parachute...and meditate. It not only improves your mind, it mends your body and your soul as well.

"In its presence we can remember something beyond the moment, a strength on which to build a life. Silence is a place of great power and healing." ...Rachel Naomi Remen

Can you feel it? Can you sense it? Can you almost touch it? Yes. The prison walls are coming down. You are now seeing the corruption that has enslaved all of humanity...start to implode.

Whether you like it or not, the world is changing. We are transitioning into a whole new earth. And, the fact that so many people have started to awaken, even when everything was stacked against us, is a miracle unto itself.

So, now the real journey begins. There are tools out there to help you all do this. The work is simple, but it's not easy.

Think with your hearts. You know in your soul what is truth. Start to listen to those whispers, those nigglings that are questionable. For, you are on a difficult path in this time of change...you must negotiate your way through deceit, confusion and downright lies.

If you are feeling tired, sick, overwhelmed and angry...including anger directed at me for mentioning this, then you are experiencing exactly what has allowed this power to work for so long. And, why it is so necessary to get "real" with yourself, to sit quietly and ask the important questions. Let yourself be released from the shackles of your mind, let those blindfolds drop away and see the world as it is, not as you are being told it is.

In your silence, start creating a peaceful world. A loving world. In your silence...start trusting yourself. It is there you will see your power and your healing. Guidance is available. You need only ask.

"If every word I said could make you laugh, I'd talk forever."
...The Beach Boys

Laughter is oh, so good medicine. What's more, it's a genuine way of elevating our own natural vibrational set-point and clearing any toxic energy within our body. Laughter is oh, so good for the soul.

You see, we spend so much time looking externally for happiness and abundance that is somehow never sustained. There never seems to be enough and we generally feel as if we are living in a state of lack.

As a wise seer once said, "No one ever needs to suffer as there is an ocean of bliss in everyone." If we just embraced a daily practice of quieting our minds, and connecting to the deep ocean within us, very soon we would be experiencing an overflow. That is how powerful stilling your mind is!

If you do this on a regular basis, you will find that you can no longer hold back the bliss, the laughter, the love that is within you. That laughter will bubble up from deep inside and erupt out of you like a tidal wave that cannot be held back. And, you will have a natural urge to share your happiness, your compassion, your giving nature with others in their time of need. Still feeling complete and fulfilled yourself!

I think you already feel it but a HUGE wave of LAUGHTER is coming your way. Belly roll please...

"TRANSITION"

"Be quiet my soul, be quiet. Let the waves take you one by one and sail you to the crescent of the moon.

Yes, the world is roaring and there is work to do...but tonight, my soul, tonight is yours to behold.

The beauty of a December sunset as the year prepares to yield and take its place in history."

...Unknown

Through all of this busy-ness we call life...in this insanity-filled world...my wish for you is stillness for Your soul. My desire is that you find love for Yourself. My dream is that you find peace in Your heart. May you be empowered to seek the joy in life You deserve.

My dream for you Begin. Within.

"Noise is a cruel ruler who is always imposing curfews. While stillness and quiet break open the vintage bottles, and awake the real Band."
...Hafiz

Quiet time each day is sooooo important. The trouble is, it can be unnerving to sit in stillness for many people as they're out of practice. We spend so much of our lives looking externally for happiness and abundance when all along there is an ocean of bliss just sitting there inside us waiting to be discovered.

If you start to embrace a daily practice of quieting the mind, and connect to that deep ocean within you, you will eventually experience a Band unlike anything you've ever heard before. A Band that will explode in a symphony of bliss. "Rock me Amadeus." "You Can't Always Get What You Want, But You Just Might Find....you get what you need."

It is then that you won't be able to hold back the happiness, the joy, the love within you. It will be like a wave rushing over you and you will just naturally want to give, to share, and to help humanity any way you can.

So brave that void if you dare, where darkness is the greatest. Trust the stillness. Embrace the quiet. Feel the calm. And, anticipate that emotional rush of jubilation. This is the power of a Calm Moment.

38620017R00115

Made in the USA
Charleston, SC
14 February 2015